# Digging and Discovery
# Wisconsin Archaeology

## 2nd Edition

Diane Young Holiday, PhD

Bobbie Malone, PhD

Wisconsin Historical Society Press

www.wisconsinhistory.org/whspress

Photographs identified with PH, WHi, or WHS are from the Society's collections; address inquiries about such photos to the Visual Materials Archivist at the above address.

Publications of the Wisconsin Historical Society Press are available at quantity discounts for promotions, fund raising, and educational use. Write to the above address for more information.

Printed in the United States of America

Cover and text design by Jill Bremigan

09 08 07 06 05     1 2 3 4 5

Library of Congress Cataloging-in-Publication Data

Holliday, Diane Young, 1951-
  Digging and discovery : Wisconsin archaeology /
Diane Young Holliday, Bobbie Malone.-- 2nd ed.
      p. cm.
  Includes bibliographical references and index.
  ISBN-13: 978-0-87020-376-3 (pbk. : alk. paper)
  ISBN-10: 0-87020-376-2 (pbk. : alk. paper)
1. Wisconsin--Antiquities--Juvenile literature. 2. Excavations (Archaeology)--Wisconsin--Juvenile literature. 3. Indians of North America--Wisconsin--Antiquities--Juvenile literature. I. Malone, Bobbie, 1944- II. State Historical Society of Wisconsin. III. Title.
F583.H65 2006
977.5'01--dc22

                                        2006004892

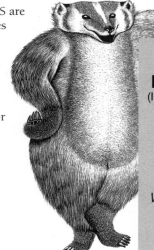

## Other Titles in the New Badger History Series
(Includes classroom texts and teacher guides)

*Voices & Votes*
*How Democracy Works in Wisconsin*

*Learning from the Land:*
*Wisconsin Land Use*

*Working with Water: Wisconsin Waterways*

*They Came to Wisconsin*

*Native People of Wisconsin*

∞ The paper used in this publication meets the minimum requirements of the American National Standard for Information Sciences—Permanence of Paper for Printed Library Materials, ANSI Z39.48-1992.

# Digging and Discovery
## Wisconsin Archaeology

# Contents

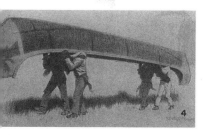

# Introduction

In *Digging and Discovery: Wisconsin Archaeology* you will learn 2 main ideas. First, you will learn about Wisconsin's **ancient** (**ayn** chunt) and not so ancient past. Second, you will find out how **archaeologists** (ar kee **ol** uh jists) learn about this past from the things people left behind. The evidence that archaeologists find can tell us about the people who moved into Wisconsin as the glaciers melted. Archaeologists also find out about the people who came into our state 10,000 years later to work in lead mines and logging camps.

*This archaelogist is taking notes to document what he has discovered.*

Once you learn how archaeologists work and what they have discovered about Wisconsin's history, you will know more than most adults about archaeology in our state! You will also understand the importance of protecting our past.

In this book, we tell the story of Wisconsin as we know it through **archaeology** (ar kee **ol** uh jee). Archaeology is learning about past people by studying what they left in the places where they once lived.

**ancient:** Very old

We begin with the oldest known places where humans lived, worked, and worshipped. Then we travel through time to learn about more recent people and events. The story covers over 10,000 years—from the butchering of mammoths, to the first villages, to railroads and logging camps.

Archaeologists are interested in learning about all people in the past, where and how people lived, and how these past lives and events have influenced our world today. You will learn how archaeologists **excavate** (**ex** cuh vate), **document**, **analyze**, and report what they find. Does this sound like something you'd like to do? Maybe one day you will be an archaeologist!

**excavate:** Carefully dig     **document:** Write down and/or photograph     **analyze:** Carefully study

# Chapter 1

## Pathways to the Past

◆ ◆ ◆

Who are you? Why do you talk and act the way you do? An Italian, sailing under a Spanish flag, supposedly "discovered" North America. But hundreds of Indian

WHi (X3) 2306

*What clues about the past can you find in this historical photograph? Who do you think these people are? When do you think they lived in Wisconsin? Do you think their lives were easier or harder than yours today?*

Nations—speaking their own languages—lived here. So why do most people in Wisconsin speak English every day? To understand ourselves, we have to know our past.

There are many ways to learn about the past. You can ask your grandparents or older friends to describe what their lives were like when they were your age. You might also look at old photographs, read history books, or visit historical museums. But most of our past was never photographed, never written down, and is no longer in people's memories. Archaeology is a way to learn about this past.

## Think About It

What is archaeology? How do archaeologists learn about the past? How do they tell how old things are? How do they know where to dig? How do they excavate sites? What do they do with the things they find?

# How Do Archaeologists Learn About the Past?

Archaeologists learn about past people by studying **artifacts** (**ar** tih fax) or objects left behind at places where people lived, worked, and played. They also study **features**, immovable human-made things, like house foundations. Archaeologists often display the artifacts they collect in museums. But these objects have other, more important uses.

Archaeologists use the artifacts and features to **hypothesize** (hi **poth** uh size) about the lives of the people who made and used them.

By examining an artifact, an archaeologist can learn about past **technology** (teck **nol** uh gee) and even learn about travel and trade. For example, some stone tools that archaeologists have found in Wisconsin are made from Knife River **chalcedony** (kal **sed** uh nee). This is a type of stone only found hundreds of miles away in North Dakota. That stone didn't walk here by itself! Either it was traded through groups of people living between here and North Dakota, or somebody took a very long hike.

**DID YOU KNOW?**

Hypothesizing is part of science. Scientists decide how or why they think something might have happened. This idea is called a hypothesis. Scientists then test this **hypothesis** by collecting information and seeing whether this information fits their idea or not. If the information does not fit their idea, they change their hypothesis and test again by collecting more information. Through this process, scientists hope to get closer and closer to what really happened.

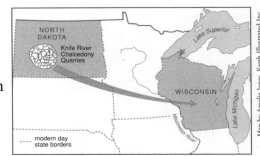

*Map by Amelia Janes, Earth Illustrated Inc.*

*Chalcedony came from North Dakota, a long way from Wisconsin. How do you think it got here thousands of years ago?*

**hypothesize:** Come up with an idea to test with evidence   **technology:** How things were made

By examining an artifact and other artifacts or features found with it, archaeologists also try to re-create what happened at a particular place and time. For example, suppose a volcano erupted on your playground (*very unlikely* here in Wisconsin!) and suddenly covered your school in 10 feet of volcanic ash. If, 3,000 years in the future, archaeologists looked at what was left in your classroom, what would they find? Do you think that these archaeologists could tell that the building was a school? What type of artifacts might they find? Would these artifacts be good clues?

What if 3,000 years from now there are no schools like there are today, and the archaeologists don't know what schools used to look like? Would the archaeologists still be able to determine that the building was a school instead of a factory, or a church, or a department store? Would there be any artifacts or features that would tell them that mainly children used the building?

**DID YOU KNOW?**

Artifacts include items like tin cans, stone arrowheads, pottery, jewelry, and nails. All of these are objects made by *people*. Archaeologists look at objects such as these and learn about past groups of people.

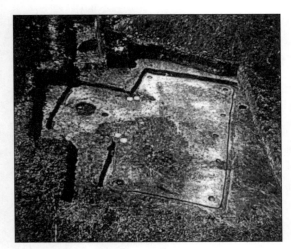
*House foundation from 1000 years ago*

Archaeologists call any place of past human activity a **site**. An archaeological site can be an Indian village like Tremaine, occupied about 300 to 700 years ago. Or it can be a small Euro-American town like Williamsonville. Loggers built this Door County town in the late 1860s, but the Great Peshtigo Fire destroyed it in 1871. An archaeological site can also be a shipwreck on the bottom of Lake Superior. Or a site can be just a few scattered fragments of stone tools, thrown away or lost by families living along the Mississippi River thousands of years ago.

*Archaeologists use the same careful methods, whether they are investigating house remains from an Indian village 1000 years old or from a farm house 150 years old.*

*House foundation from 150 years ago*

Williamsonville

Tremaine

Every archaeological site has its own story to tell about past life in Wisconsin.

## How Old Is It?

To hypothesize about the age of the sites and the artifacts and features, archaeologists use dating methods. Dating methods help archaeologists figure out how old things are. Sometimes archaeologists can get *absolute* dates, meaning an exact year like AD 800 or 800 BC. *AD* means *Anno Domini*, a Christian term in Latin for "Year of Our Lord." *BC* simply means Before Christ. In Western culture, this is the common way to show dates for different years. Other cultures have different ways of showing dates.

Radiocarbon dating is one type of test that can tell the exact age of an artifact. Archaeologists also use *relative* dating methods. This means that an archaeologist can be sure that one artifact is older than another but can't tell exactly how old they are.

### DID YOU KNOW?

All living things take in a chemical element called carbon. Some of this carbon is a form called carbon 14. It is radioactive, which means that carbon gives off tiny particles called electrons at a known rate— half of it **decays** and disappears every 5,730 years! Once a living thing dies, no more carbon 14 is taken in, and what was there begins to decay. Because scientists know the rate of decay, they can figure out how many years have passed since a living thing has died. Scientists can use radiocarbon dating on things like corn, bone, and burned wood from fireplaces because all of these were once alive. Radiocarbon does not work on objects like rocks or pottery.

**decays:** Rots away

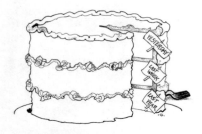

Archaeologists recover artifacts one layer at a time. Most often, the deeper the artifact is found, the older it is.

One method of relative dating is based on how deep artifacts and features are found in the ground. It's like a layer cake. The baker puts the bottom layer on the plate first and covers it with frosting before adding more layers. Through time, nature can cover artifacts, gradually burying them with thousands of years of dust or quickly with volcanic ash or mud from flooding rivers. In places where artifacts are getting buried, the oldest artifacts are found at the deepest levels. That's because they were buried first. That means that archaeologists find the oldest artifacts last, since they are at the bottom of the dig.

## How Do Archaeologists Find Sites?

To look for evidence at a site, archaeologists systematically dig small holes, called "shovel testing." Why is this an important method?

One of the easiest ways to find a site in Wisconsin is to walk over a plowed field. If you see broken pieces of pottery or an arrowhead, or bricks and old bottles, you have found an archaeological site. Teams of archaeologists walk over fields in a **systematic** (sis tem **at** tic) way, making sure that they examine the whole field. One common method archaeologists use is to spread out in a row about 30 feet apart from one another and walk in the same direction. In places where grass covers the ground surface, archaeologists will look for buried

**systematic:** Carefully planned

artifacts by systematically digging small holes. Archaeologists will then make a map of the place where they found the artifacts. The archaeologists hope to see patterns where particular things are found. Such patterns can help archaeologists decide what happened at a site.

## How Do Archaeologists Excavate and Document?

After discovering a site, archaeologists may decide to excavate portions of it. Excavating helps them learn more exactly when the site was occupied, and what the people were doing there. Archaeologists have to carefully keep track of exactly where they find everything, both horizontally and vertically. That's why they only dig a few inches at a time, always down to the same level across the **excavation unit** .

*Archaeologists must work slowly and carefully when they excavate a site.*

**excavation unit:** Rectangular area dug by archaeologists

**FEATURE SHEET**

p. _____ of _____

Site No. 47 LC 95    Site Name: TREMAINE Unit: S120 E175    Fea. # 26

Location in Unit (center) northwest corner Level/Depth. -35 cm _____ gs/d

Surface Appearance: dark, sharply defined circular stain

Horizontal Shape: circular

Horizontal Size: 1.0 meter x 1.10 meter (Note Direction)

Vertical Shape: steep-walled    Vertical Thickness: 1.25 meters

(NOTE: Describe variation in thickness, appearance): steep vertical walls and a flat base

Samples Taken(circle): (Float) (C 14) Phytolith    Soil    Bag Number(s): 93-75, 76

Describe Matrix (e.g., Texture vs non-feature soil, contents, MUNSELL COLOR):

sandy   10YR 3/2

Contents: 15 sherds (all midway incised types), 3 fish bones, 12 mammal bones, fire-cracked rock, tip of triangular point, scraper + flakes

Relationship to other features: this pit is located at the south end of House 5, just west of feature 25

Photo: (Y) or N Plan:    Color Roll # 16    Exp. # 3-4    B & W Roll # 16    Exp. # 5-6

Y or (N) Profile:    Color Roll # ___    Exp. # ___    B & W Roll # ___    Exp. # ___

Maps Drawn:    Plan View: (Y) or N    Vertical Profile: (Y) or N

Comments: storage pit, re-used for refuse?, artifacts + bone concentrated at base of pit

Excavators: _____    Recorder: _____

Date Started: 6/8/93    Date Completed: 6/8/93

Archaeologists keep careful notes to document their findings.

**WHAT IS THAT?**

A **trowel** is a tool used to carefully scrape back dirt.

A **paintbrush** is a tool used to carefully remove dirt from fragile artifacts.

A **chaining pin** is a tool used to mark places on sites.

By sifting dirt through a screen, archaeologists can find small artifacts.

Archaeologists carefully sift the dirt through a screen so that they can find even the smallest artifacts. Excavation units are generally rectangular pits, often about a yard or 2 wide. Working within these units, archaeologists map and photograph *everything* they find. This includes artifacts and features, such as garbage pits and house foundations.

Archaeologists must document everything because when a site is excavated it is also being destroyed! If an archaeologist does not keep careful records, valuable information on **context** is lost forever. Context is the most important clue to the way the artifact or feature was used.

Even with the most careful documentation, however, archaeologists can never record everything that was at the site. Many objects rot away before any archaeologist sees them! This sometimes makes an archaeologist's job difficult. It's like trying to put together a jigsaw puzzle without having most of the pieces and without knowing what the final picture is supposed to look like!

## Back in the Laboratory

Digging is only a small part of an archaeologist's job. After the excavation is over, archaeologists must analyze what they found. Then they write reports, give tours and speeches, and develop Web materials to share the information with others.

**context:** Exactly where artifacts are found and what is found with them

Archaeologists must also wash and label artifacts with all the exact information about where they were found. This part of the work takes a lot of time. But this documenting is necessary because other archaeologists may wish to use these same artifacts in future research. Carefully preparing and storing artifacts is called **curation** (cyur **a** shun).

*This is a piece of a bowl made from a turtle's shell. After archaeologists found the shell, they curated it for future generations.*

Remember that 10 feet of volcanic ash? If that ash also buried your house or apartment building, what patterns of artifacts would future archaeologists see? Would they find plates and bowls in every room? What might archaeologists learn about you from the artifacts found in your room? Would archaeologists find out something different from artifacts found in your kitchen?

In the other chapters of this book you'll find what archaeologists have discovered about the past 12,000 years in the land that we call Wisconsin. Do you think it will still be called "Wisconsin" in another 12,000 years? Do you think the land will have changed? Will people have changed? How do *you* think you will be remembered?

## Looking Back

Like history, archaeology is a way to learn about the past. Historians study documents like newspapers, letters, paintings, and photographs to learn about the past. But most of the day-to-day events of the past were never photographed or written down. So archaeologists look at how people lived their everyday lives by studying the things that people left behind. The artifacts and features that archaeologists find at a specific site provide clues about the way people there used to live, work, worship, and play many years ago.

Through careful excavation and analysis, archaeologists can learn how old an archaeological site is and how life changed over time for the different groups of people who lived in that same place. Archaeology is a very important tool to help us learn about the past and ourselves.

# Chapter 2

## When Great Furry Beasts Roamed the Land

◆ ◆ ◆

If you don't have a down jacket or a home with a furnace, it's not easy living near the edge of a **glacier** (**gla** shur), a sheet of ice sometimes hundreds of feet wide. When people moved into Wisconsin between 11,000 and 12,000 years ago, that's basically what they did. Archaeologists call the first people in Wisconsin, and all of North America, **Paleo-Indians** .

## Think About It

When did people first come to Wisconsin? What was the environment like? What were these first people like? What do we know about them?

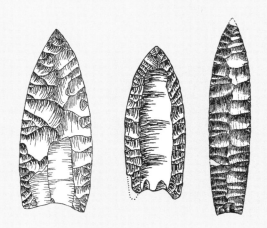

# A Different Environment

When the Paleo-Indians arrived, parts of northern Wisconsin were covered with glaciers, sheets of ice that were sometimes hundreds of feet thick. The glaciers formed when huge amounts of snow piled up, so much snow that its weight created enough force to turn the snow into sheets of ice.

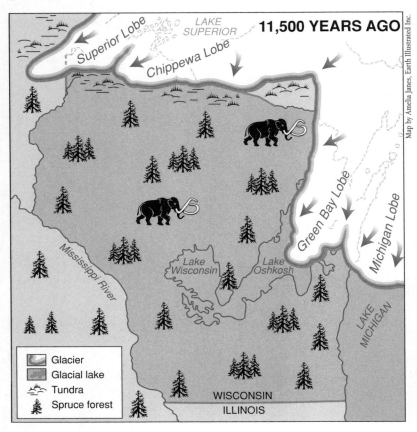

Glacier ice is not like the ice in your freezer. The great pressure that it is under gives glacier ice special qualities. Glacier ice can flow, sometimes only a few inches in a year, sometimes hundreds of feet in a year. It all depends on how much snow falls and how cold it is.

*Compare this map of Wisconsin to one today. You can see how much of Wisconsin was still covered by ice and glacial lakes 11,500 years ago. It was much colder then. What kinds of plants could survive?*

Map by Amelia Janes, Earth Illustrated Inc.

16

The weather was colder and wetter when the Paleo-Indians lived here. That long ago, Wisconsin was home to many animals that are **extinct** or no longer exist, such as 2 early members of the elephant family— **mammoths** and **mastodons** (**mas** tuh dons)—and giant beavers. Wisconsin did not look the way it does now. No barns, no roads, no corn, no cows, no cheese! Even the locations and levels of lakes and rivers were different. Some were higher, some were lower, and some didn't exist yet. Archaeologists try to determine what the land looked like thousands of years ago so they can figure out likely areas where people might have camped or hunted.

## Paleo-Indian Life

So far, archaeologists have found very few sites that are 11,000 to 12,000 years old. That's why we know so little about the Paleo-Indian people. From the few sites that have been found, archaeologists hypothesize that Paleo-Indians lived in small family groups and traveled a lot. That means, these family groups stayed only a short amount of time at any particular place. They were hunters and gatherers. They spent most of their time tracking and hunting animals and gathering wild plants. That's the way they survived.

*Wisconsin was once home to mammoths like the one pictured here.*

## The Importance of Tools

We learn about the Paleo-Indians mainly through their stone tools. Archaeologists know that the Paleo-Indians hunted because they left behind stone spear points. Stone tools are one of the few artifacts that can survive for long periods of time, even thousands of years.

Paleo-Indians made very **distinctive** (dis **tink** tihv) stone spear points. When archaeologists find one of these spear points, they know that they have a Paleo-Indian site. Unfortunately, in Wisconsin most Paleo-Indian spear points have been found on the ground's surface without other artifacts. Without other artifacts for context, it is difficult to explain what happened at a site. Did a Paleo-Indian use a spear point to kill a mammoth or an elk? Was the spear point used to kill anything at all? Archaeologists need more context. An artifact that we find all by itself cannot tell us much about how or why someone originally used it.

*Paleo-Indians needed to hunt for nearly all their food.*

For example, if you found an old rusty knife in the woods, what could you say about the person who had used it or why it happened to be in that particular place? Was this the scene of a battle? Was the knife simply lost by a hiker? Was this the location of an early farm site? Without more information, it is difficult to know what that knife means. However, if archaeologists dig excavation

**distinctive:** Easy to identify

units near the knife's location and discover tin cans, a rusty fork, broken dishes, and the remains of a cellar, they would then be able to conclude that this was an early house site.

While it is very important to find artifacts in context, archaeologists can also get information from a single artifact. If, for example, that knife found in the woods was a modern Swiss Army knife, we would know that it didn't come from an early homestead, and we could hypothesize that a hiker simply lost the knife. By being familiar with types of artifacts from the past, an archaeologist can make a hypothesis from a single artifact.

A Paleo-Indian spear point found in a Richland County cornfield tells us that people were at that spot 10,000 to 12,000 years ago. Examining the spear point can also tell us how Paleo-Indians made stone tools and even help "date" them. For example, **fluted points** are older than other kinds of Paleo-Indian points. Archaeologists know this because they have found some fluted and unfluted points in context and with materials that were radiocarbon dated.

Examining the spear point may also tell us about Paleo-Indian travel and trade. That spear point in Richland County might be made of Knife River chalcedony, the stone found only in North Dakota!

*The shape of these spear points and the way they were made offer clues to their age.*

*Clovis point (fluted) 9,000 BC*

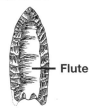

*Folsom point (fluted) 8,500 BC*

*Agate Basin point 8,000 BC*

**fluted points:** Spear points with large grooves running up from bottom of point, used by Paleo-Indians

## But Can We Learn More?

People of the past were, of course, more than just the tools they used or the food they ate. However, if only a few artifacts are available, it is difficult for archaeologists to figure out what people thought about or believed. Archaeologists have not yet been able to learn much about the beliefs of Paleo-Indians, but they have found clues. For example, at 2 sites in Wisconsin—one in Price County and the other in Brown County—archaeologists found finely made stone spear points that Paleo-Indians had burned on purpose. Archaeologists hypothesize that the Paleo-Indians had deliberately burned them because the spear points were in very small pieces, broken up from intense heat. Why did the Paleo-Indians burn these points? Could this action have been part of a religious **ceremony** (**ser** uh mo nee)? Archaeologists can only hypothesize and hope to find more data to answer these questions.

## Kenosha County Mammoths— Believe It or Not

In 1964, a Kenosha County farmer was digging a ditch in a low-lying field and discovered mammoth-sized bones. Amazingly, they *were* actual mammoth bones! These bones, a **femur** (fe mur) and part of a tusk, were taken to the Kenosha County Public Museum. There they sat for almost 30 years. In 1992, an archaeologist researching Paleo-Indians examined these bones. He noticed cutmarks that could only have been made by human beings. This was a very important discovery

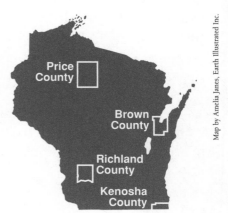

**ceremony:** Formal words, actions, or songs that mark an important occasion, such as a wedding or funeral
**femur:** Thigh bone

because it proved that people had been at this site between 10,000 and 12,000 years ago.

Archaeologists hoped to learn more about Paleo-Indian life. So they decided to return to the area where the farmer had uncovered the mammoth bones and carefully excavate the rest of the site. Fortunately, in 1964 someone had made a map of the site, and the archaeologists were able to find the right spot. Archaeologists opened up a series of excavation units. Gradually they uncovered bones of an adult male mammoth. The archaeologists did not find any spear points that would definitely prove that Paleo-Indians had killed the animal. But they did find a broken stone tool. They also saw cutmarks on the bones that indicated that Paleo-Indians had definitely butchered the animal.

*What clues do you see that tell you archaeologists are beginning their excavation for the mammoth bones in a Kenosha Country cornfield?*

*People butchering a mastodon*

Image courtesy of the Kentucky Heritage Council. Artist: Jimmy Railey

21

Since this discovery in Kenosha County, archaeologists have continued work in this same area. They wanted to learn more about Paleo-Indian life and the past environment of southeastern Wisconsin. They found a second mammoth site less than a mile from the first one. This second site also had a stone tool with it. Archaeologists examined the types of dirt in the excavation units and surrounding landscape. They learned that both of these mammoths died on the edge of a former lake.

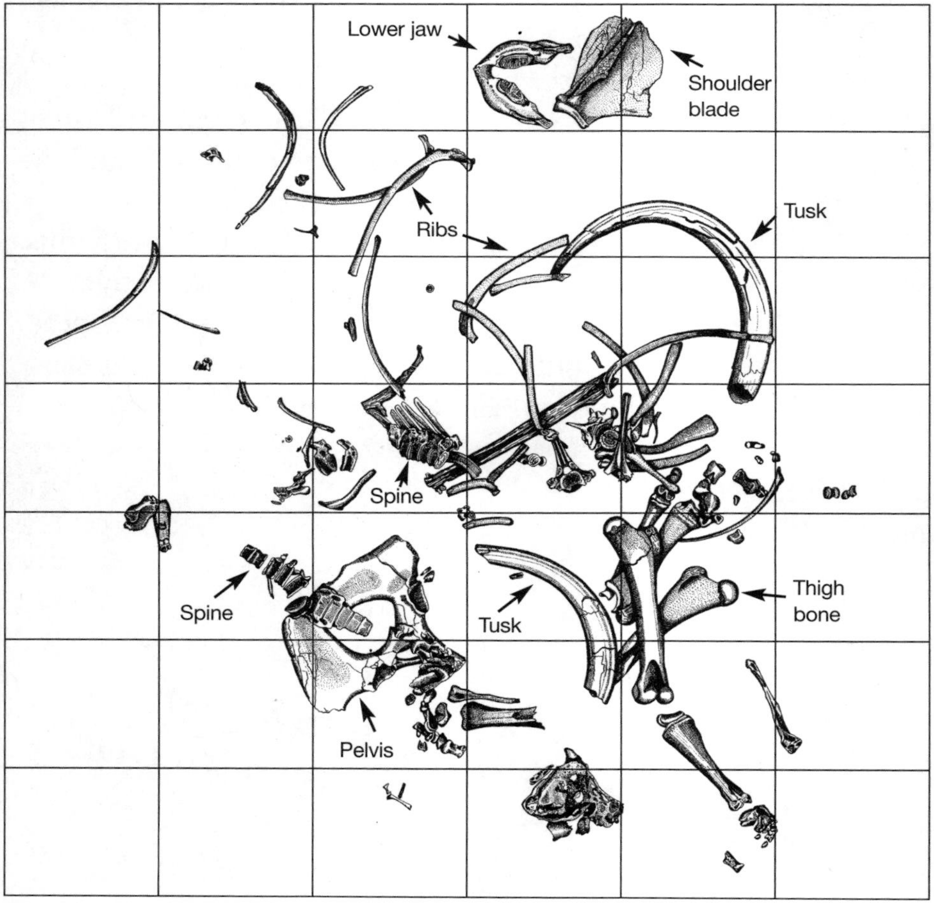

Lower jaw
Shoulder blade
Ribs
Tusk
Spine
Spine
Tusk
Thigh bone
Pelvis


Courtesy of the Great Lakes Archaeological Research Center

*This map of mammoth bones in Kenosha County shows exactly where archaeologists found the bones at one site.*

Although these mammoth kill sites or butchering sites are exciting to find, archaeologists need to know more. They also need information from different types of sites so they can better understand how Paleo-Indians lived. That is why archaeologists were very excited to find a Paleo-Indian campsite within a couple of miles of the mammoth sites. They do not know if these campers were the same people who butchered the mammoths. But archaeologists do know that the types of stone tools found at the campsite date to the same time period when mammoths lived.

Archaeologists carefully recorded a number of features at the campsite. These features included **hearths** (harths) and places that held many stone tools and burned bones. Archaeologists who study animal bones will be able to tell what these people were eating. Maybe they ate mammoth or deer or both! Perhaps most importantly, archaeologists may have found the remains of a small house. More study of other features at this site may help archaeologists tell if a single small family kept coming back to this same place over many years. Or maybe several families all came to this place at the same time.

## Mammoths and Mastodons

Mammoths are extinct today. But thousands of years ago, they roamed the Northern Hemisphere from Siberia to Arizona. Unlike modern elephants, mammoths were covered with long, coarse hair. In fact, people often call them "wooly mammoths." Fully grown males had long, twisted tusks. Their **molars** , or chewing teeth, were wide and relatively flat.

**hearths:** Fire pits

**Paleontologists** (pa le uhn **tol** uh jists) know that mammoths ate large amounts of grass, moss, and occasionally parts of trees. Paleontologists learned this information from studying the stomach contents of frozen mammoths that they found **intact** in Siberia in Asia.

Mastodons are another extinct mammal related to the elephant. Their teeth are quite different from mammoths'. Instead of shallow grooves, the chewing surfaces of their teeth were pointed, better for chopping soft grass. Because mastodon teeth are so different from mammoth teeth, paleontologists think that the mastodon's diet and preferred places to live must have been different from the mammoth's. Unlike the grass-eating wooly mammoths, mastodons ate herbs, shrubs, and trees. Mastodons probably lived in forested areas.

The mammoth and mastodon became extinct in North America at about the same time people first arrived. That's why some archaeologists have argued about whether *people* were responsible for their extinction. Several of the early famous Paleo-Indian sites were mammoth kills. Did the Paleo-Indians kill too many? Other archaeologists argue that the mammoths' disappearance also occurred at the same time as the end of the glaciers. This was a time when many other animals—types that people did *not* hunt—also became extinct. These archaeologists suggest that climate change led to the extinction of the mammoths and mastodons.

*Mastodon skull*

**paleontologists:** Scientists who study ancient animals and plants
**intact:** Whole

## Looking Back

Based on the archaeological evidence, people first lived in Wisconsin between 11,000 and 12,000 years ago. Archaeologists call the first people Paleo-Indians. Wisconsin was a very different place back then. The glaciers were melting and shrinking back, but it was still colder than today. Very different plants and animals—including some that are now extinct—like mammoths and mastodons, filled the landscape.

Paleo-Indians lived in small family groups and hunted and gathered their foods. They probably moved their camps often in search of food. Because few Paleo-Indian sites and artifacts survived and have been found, there is still much to learn about these first people.

# Chapter 3

# Archaic People: Hunters and Gatherers

◆ ◆ ◆

Six thousand years is a *really* long time. In fact, it's about 30 times the age of the United States of America! Yet, for about *6,000* years—between approximately 6500 and 800 BC—Wisconsin was home to people whom archaeologists call **Archaic** (ar **kay** ic) Indians. Archaeologists also call this whole time period the Archaic!

We do not know the number of people who lived in Wisconsin during these years, or the number of groups these people formed, or the names these groups chose to call themselves. We *do* know more about Archaic people than about Paleo-Indians because Archaic people left behind more artifacts and sites. And based on the greater number of sites, archaeologists hypothesize that the population in Wisconsin had greatly increased during those 6,000 years.

WHi (X3) 50542

*Deer became an important source of food.*

## Think About It

How did the environment change after the glaciers disappeared? Did Archaic people live differently than Paleo-Indians? How do archaeologists know this? What kinds of new tools have archaeologists found?

*Archaic Indians used new hunting weapons to kill deer.*

*Archaic people lived in villages, but they moved as the seasons changed. Why do you think they moved during the year?*

# Changing Times

We know that during the Archaic years Wisconsin experienced many changes, both in the environment and in the people who lived here. During this 6,000 years, the climate was getting warmer and drier. The glaciers that had once blanketed much of Wisconsin were long gone.

At first, pine forests covered much of Wisconsin. When the climate continued to warm, the pine forests grew well only in northern Wisconsin's cooler temperatures. Oak forests, like we see today, began to thrive in warmer southern Wisconsin. The animals changed, too. The caribou and moose followed the pines northward, while the mammoths and mastodons disappeared forever. In the southern part of the state, smaller game now roamed.

**DID YOU KNOW?**

Archaeologists believe that Archaic people settled in some areas. Or people traveled shorter distances and returned to the same areas regularly.

Archaic people **adapted** (uh **dap** ted) to this warming environment. From the types of animal bones excavated at Archaic campsites, archaeologists know that Archaic people hunted smaller game like elk, deer, rabbits, and birds and that they also fished.

Archaic people also continued to gather plants. And, as the climate warmed, more varieties of plants became available. At Archaic sites, archaeologists found different types of tools used to prepare food and medicines. Based on these new tools, they think that Archaic people used more varieties of plants than Paleo-Indians did.

**adapted:** Changed because of a new situation

# New Tools, New Tasks

Archaic people began to make totally new kinds of tools like stone axes and grinding stones. These newer tools are called **groundstone** tools, because they were formed by someone grinding one stone against a harder stone. These new kinds of tools suggest that people were doing different kinds of work, like chopping down trees and smashing and grinding nuts and seeds.

This drawing shows the way an Archaic Indian woman ground nuts and seeds between 2 stones.

Archaic people also continued to make spear points for hunting. But these points had different shapes than those made by Paleo-Indians. Archaic points usually have notches at the bottoms; Paleo-Indian points don't. This means that Archaic people probably attached spear points to the spear shafts in different ways than Paleo-Indians did.

What kind of work could Archaic Indians do with a stone axe like this one?

Archaic people also developed other new ways of doing old things. One of their inventions may have been the **atlatl** (at ul at ul). The atlatl is a special tool that helps people throw a spear farther and more forcefully than they could with just their arms. The Paleo-Indians may have also used atlatls, but archaeologists have not found evidence of atlatls in Wisconsin until the Archaic period.

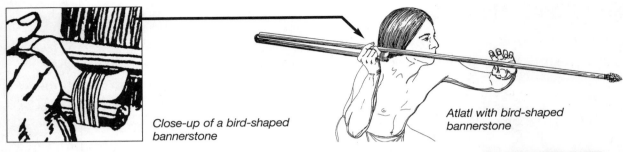

*Close-up of a bird-shaped bannerstone*

*Atlatl with bird-shaped bannerstone*

At some Archaic sites, archaeologists have found highly polished **bannerstones** . These pieces of stone, some worked into the shapes of animals, were probably used as handles or weights on the atlatls. This extra weight causes the spear to fly faster and farther.

### DID YOU KNOW?

Archaeologists have not yet discovered the remains of any Archaic houses in Wisconsin. They think that Archaic people lived in shelters made of branches, hides and mats. Archaic Indians sometimes found shelter in caves, much the same way as Paleo-Indians did.

## New Materials, Too

Archaic people also began to make their tools from different materials, like copper. Between about 3000 and 1200 BC, some people started using copper to make tools for hunting, fishing, and woodworking. Tens of thousands of these tools have been found in Wisconsin, mainly on the surface of the ground in the eastern half of the state. Chemical studies of the copper indicate that much of it comes from the Upper Peninsula (UP) of Michigan. The UP has places where nearly pure copper lay on the ground surface or was just shallowly buried. Archaeologists who have **surveyed** (**sur** vayd) in the UP have found thousands of pits where Archaic people **quarried**  (**kwor** eed) this copper.

**surveyed:** Looked for artifacts or features    **quarried:** Dug out

Archaeologists have much to learn about the "Old Copper" people who made and used these copper tools. Although archaeologists have found thousands of Old Copper tools in Wisconsin, most of the tools were on the surface. These Old Copper tools were not found with other artifacts or features.

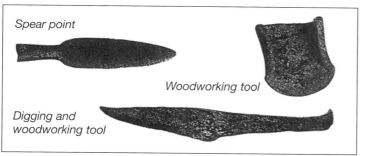

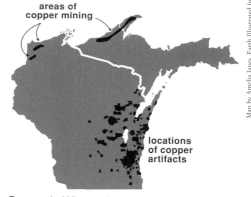

areas of copper mining

locations of copper artifacts

Copper in Wisconsin

Spear point

Woodworking tool

Digging and woodworking tool

"Old Copper" people shaped copper into tools to use and trade.

Without other clues, it is difficult for archaeologists to tell how the Old Copper people lived their lives, or even if there was a single group of people that can be called the Old Copper people. Perhaps several groups of very different people used copper to make tools during Archaic times. In order to get a better idea of what Old Copper really was, archaeologists need to find and investigate many village and campsites. Then they could discover how the people who made these copper tools lived.

Map by Amelia Janes, Earth Illustrated Inc.

Bass
Site

There were no hardware stores 8,000 years ago. There were no factories to produce steel, aluminum, or plastic. If you needed a tool, you made a tool, using copper, bone, wood, or stone. And not just any stone would do.

It takes particular kinds of rock to make good grinding stones. It takes other kinds of stone to make good spear points or knives. Stone tools were the best (and sometimes the *only*) tools available for particular tasks. So it was very important for people to know where they could get the right kind of stone. About 8,000 years ago, Archaic people found such a place in Grant County in southwestern Wisconsin. Archaeologists have named this place the Bass site.

## The Bass Quarry Site: Tools Are Us

Thousands of years ago, at the end of glacial times, it was still wetter and cooler than today. Water wearing away the soil exposed **bedrock** and large chunks of **chert**, an excellent rock for making spear points. This chert lay exposed at the Bass site for about a thousand years. During this time, Archaic people regularly came to the site, leaving behind over 75,000 artifacts!

Image courtesy of the Kentucky Heritage Council
Artist: Jimmy Railey

*Man making tool*

32    **bedrock:** The solid rock that lies underneath soils

Archaeologists have found areas within the Bass site where people quarried pieces of rock. In other areas there, people chipped this rock into spear points and other kinds of tools. Archaeologists identified these areas by the different kinds of stone artifacts that they found in different parts of the site.

*Hardin-Barbed spear points like these were found at the Bass Site. How are they different from the Clovis, Folsom, and Agate Basin points you already saw?*

Artist: Anna Fishkin

## FLAKING PROCESS

**1**

To make a spear point, you must first break off a large **flake** of stone from a large rock, usually with another rock, called a **hammerstone** .

**2**

Then, you gradually break off smaller and smaller flakes from this large flake.

**3**

To break off these smaller and smaller flakes, people sometimes used the tips of antlers or wooden mallets.

By examining the sizes and shapes of flakes, archaeologists can tell what was happening in different parts of a site. At the Bass site, archaeologists excavated a large area and found thousands of flakes (over 63,000!), many hammerstones, and 44 spear points.

Amazingly, 38 of these spear points (that's 86.36%!) were one type, called Hardin-Barbed. Very few Hardin-Barbed spear points have been found anywhere else in the state. Archaeologists have generally found these at sites farther south, in places like Illinois and Missouri. Maybe people farther south made special trips to Wisconsin. They still do, don't they? Count those Illinois license plates!

## Looking Back

After the glaciers disappeared from Wisconsin, the environment slowly changed into the landscape we see today. Over a period of thousands of years, the Indian people in Wisconsin adapted to the changing environment. When Archaic Indians lived in Wisconsin, the climate was warmer and drier than it was for Paleo-Indians.

More Archaic Indian sites survived, so archaeologists know more about the way they lived. Archaic Indians made new tools for new tasks. They continued to hunt and gather foods, but the mastodons and mammoths were gone. Archaic Indians hunted more deer and smaller animals and also ate a greater variety of plant foods. Archaic Indians successfully adapted, and the number of people living in Wisconsin grew.

# Chapter 4

## New Ways of Living:
## Woodland, Mississippian, and the Oneota

◆ ◆ ◆

Sometime about 800 BC (nearly 3,000 years ago), Archaic people living in eastern North America began to make a number of important changes in their lives. Three of these changes were so significant that gradually they transformed the lives of Archaic people. These 3 changes were the introduction of farming, the making of pottery, and the building of special burial mounds. Of course, not all of these changes appeared at the same time and at the same place or even at the same time in different places. However, many Archaic groups gradually began to accept and use these new ways of life. Archaeologists refer to the people who followed these new ways of life as **Woodland** .

Making pottery was one of the big changes during this time period.

Over hundreds of years, some Woodland groups began living in slightly different ways from others. Some of these ways of life became distinct from what archaeologists defined as Woodland. So archaeologists decided to assign different names to these different groups. Around AD 1000 (that's about 1,000 years ago), archaeologists think that

36

at least 3 different groups of people lived in Wisconsin: the people who still generally followed the Woodland way of life as well as 2 other groups: the **Mississippians** and the **Oneota** (O nee **o** tuh). These groups may not have been the best of friends. Archaeologists think this because some Woodland and Mississippian people lived in **fortified** (for **tuh** fyd) towns, towns behind tall wooden **stockades** or walls.

## Think About It

What new ways of life did the Woodland people follow? How were they similar and different from Archaic people? Why did Woodland people build mounds? Why did some build mounds in the shapes of animals? What other groups were living in Wisconsin 1,000 years ago? How did the Woodland, Mississippian and Oneota differ from each other?

**fortified:** To make strong and safe, protected   **stockades:** A line of posts used as a defensive fence

## Woodland Lifeways

The earliest Woodland people lived much like their **ancestors** (**an** sess turs) did during Archaic times. Woodland people continued to hunt animals and gather wild plants, but they spent longer periods of time at particular places. They probably traveled within smaller areas, too. Woodland people used more plant foods, and some Woodland groups began to **cultivate** (**cul** tih vate) plants.

Can you think why anyone would want to start farming? Farming is hard work. But planting and tending your own crops offers a secure source of food, particularly if you can grow a great deal of food. Then you can save some for winter when finding food is much more difficult. Extra food could also be used for trade with other people. Through the Woodland years, many groups depended more and more on foods that they grew rather than just foods that they gathered.

*American Indian women began cultivating a new crop—corn—as the climate in Wisconsin warmed thousands of years ago. You can still find it growing as an important crop in Wisconsin today.*

**ancestors:** Family members from long ago   **cultivate:** To grow for a purpose

# A New Invention–Pottery!

In Wisconsin, archaeologists have identified the earliest Woodland sites by the presence of **pottery**, bowls and jars made of wet clay that were then **fired**. The first pottery made in Wisconsin had tall straight walls that were sometimes up to one inch thick! This pottery was very heavy and breakable, and it is hard to imagine why people started using it. Can you think of times when a clay pot would make a better container than a basket or a hollowed gourd? Gradually, over hundreds of years, people made thinner pottery, with more interesting shapes and with different designs.

People decorated pots by pressing sticks, cords, or their fingers into the soft, wet clay and making designs before it was dried and fired. People also experimented with different ingredients to make pots. Woodland people learned that it was necessary to add something to the clay, like **grit** or sand, before it was shaped and fired. Otherwise the clay would shrink and crack. The grit or sand added to the clay is called **temper**.

Pottery is very important to archaeologists because they can examine how people made and decorated pottery and then try to use this information to identify different groups of people. Who knows? Maybe future archaeologists will call us the Tupperware people!

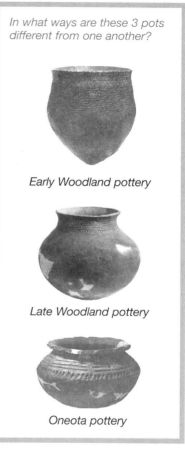

*In what ways are these 3 pots different from one another?*

*Early Woodland pottery*

*Late Woodland pottery*

*Oneota pottery*

**fired:** Hardened by heat    **grit:** Bits of rock

## New Beliefs, New Activities

It can be difficult to learn all about people's lives, particularly their beliefs, just from physical objects left behind. But Woodland features and artifacts provide many clues. Woodland people were the first to bury their dead in specially built earthen mounds. In Wisconsin, the early Woodland people built only a few burial mounds. As the years went by, however, Woodland people constructed more and more mounds.

**DID YOU KNOW?**

In past years, archaeologists excavated many American Indian burials at Wisconsin sites. Burial sites provided information about past societies. Yet archaeologists realize that many people feel that graves should not be disturbed.

In 1987, the Wisconsin Legislature passed a law to protect all human burials. Now archaeologists who wish to excavate a burial must apply for special permission from the Wisconsin Historical Society.

Between 1 BC and AD 400, a Woodland **culture** called **Hopewell** arose in the Ohio and Illinois area. Hopewell people changed ways of doing things in a large region, including parts of Wisconsin. Hopewell people constructed large burial mounds and many **earthworks**. They also made beautiful pottery and traded with people from faraway places. Even though archaeologists have collected much evidence about Hopewell culture, they are still learning what these artifacts and earthworks meant to the people who made and used them.

Hopewell people apparently honored some members of their group more than others. For example, some Hopewell people were buried with many objects, like **obsidian** (ob **sih** dee uhn) from Wyoming, large sea shells from the

culture: A group of people with shared ways of life
40    earthworks: Very large amounts of dirt formed into different shapes    obsidian: Volcanic glass

Gulf Coast, and figures cut from **mica** that came from the Appalachian Mountains. Other people in Hopewell communities were *not* buried with such fine items.

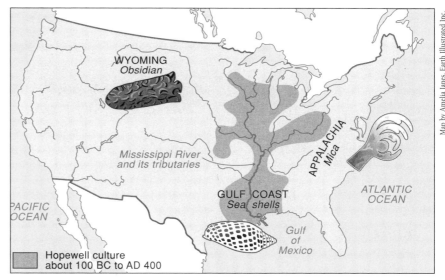

Hopewell trade objects came from far away

Archaeologists found evidence that at least some people took part in Hopewell activities, particularly in the southern areas of Wisconsin. In the early 1900s, archaeologists examined Hopewell-like burial mounds along the Mississippi River in western Wisconsin. These mounds contained burial items similar to things found in Ohio and Illinois, but not as finely made or decorated. Perhaps Wisconsin was a poorer, **frontier** area of Hopewell society, meaning that Wisconsin was just on the edges or outer boundaries of Hopewell culture.

**mica:** Shiny material

## Effigy Mounds, a Wisconsin Claim to Fame

At first, Woodland people only built burial mounds that were basically round in shape. But, starting about AD 650, some groups also built mounds in the shapes of animals, like birds and bears. These are called **effigy** (**ehf** fih jee) **mounds**. The land that we now call Wisconsin was the center of the effigy mound culture. Almost all of the known effigy mounds in the world are in the state! Only a few effigy mounds have been found in neighboring southeastern Minnesota, northeastern Iowa, and northern Illinois. Archaeologists found that people stopped building effigy mounds around AD 1200.

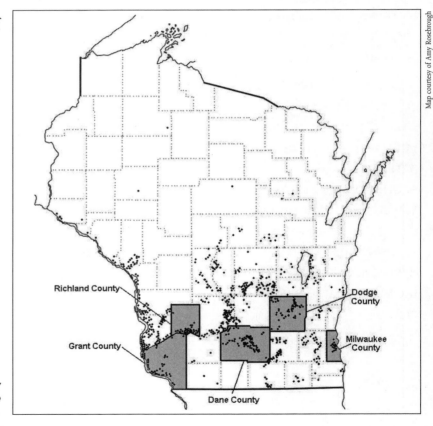

*Map courtesy of Amy Rosebrough*

*Most of the world's effigy mounds are in these Wisconsin locations.*

42

But what do effigy mounds mean? Why build a mound in the shape of an animal? Why were only a few people buried in effigy mounds? Some people suggest that the different animal shapes were

Forest Hill cemetery in Madison has a panther effigy mound behind these gravestones of more recent burials.

**spiritual** (**spir** ih chu el) symbols representing **clans** What do you think?

Panther-shaped effigy

People still use symbols today when they bury their loved ones. Wander through a cemetery. How many symbols can you recognize? If you were an archaeologist 1,000 years from now, do you think you would know what these symbols meant? We don't know why people started to build effigy mounds or why they stopped. We can only hypothesize that their beliefs changed in some way.

Gravestones tell us something about the person who died. What can you tell about this one?

spiritual: Things that have to do with the spirit    clans: Family groups with a common ancestor

43

The 3 **traditions** of the Woodland Indians—farming, pottery, and burial mounds—were important to different Woodland groups in different ways. Some Woodland groups depended upon farming. Other Woodland groups continued to rely more on hunting and gathering.

Some Woodland groups lived in relatively large towns with walls around them. Others lived in small, **unfortified** villages. Some archaeologists hypothesize that only *some* later Woodland people were building effigy mounds. By examining many Woodland sites, features, and artifacts across Wisconsin, archaeologists hope to understand more about different Woodland ways of life in our state.

## The Statz Site, a Woodland Village

Just west of Waunakee in Dane County, archaeologists found evidence of a small Woodland community. Archaeologists named this location the Statz site. People lived there between AD 700 and 1000.

The people who lived at the Statz site built 6 small houses. Part of each house was underground, and each had a long entranceway. Archaeologists call these houses **keyhole structures**. Can you guess why? So far, this particular kind of house has only been found at 3 other sites in all of Wisconsin, and these are in Dane and Dodge County!

Dodge County

Dane County

*Statz Site*

**traditions:** Ways of life   **unfortified:** Unprotected   **keyhole structures:** A small house in the shape of a keyhole

The houses at Statz are small, so archaeologists think that they were **seasonal** structures. That is, people only lived at Statz during one or 2 seasons. No one lived at the Statz site all year long. Archaeologists also think that because these houses were so small, they were occupied by small families (just parents and kids) rather than large families with grandparents, aunts, uncles, and cousins.

Woodland people lived in "keyhole" houses.

Archaeologists studied animal and plant remains hoping to figure out the season or seasons when people lived at the Statz site. For example, if a male deer skull without antlers had been found in a garbage pit, archaeologists would have known that people lived there in the winter. That's the time of year that deer shed their antlers. Unfortunately, archaeologists found very few plant or animal remains. So no one can say for sure the time of year that people lived at Statz.

People may have stayed at this site during *different* times of the year. Archaeologists found evidence, in the different layers of dirt inside the houses, that suggests that Woodland people reused each of the houses at least once.

45

Archaeologists also found small pieces of grit-tempered pottery and stone tools inside each of the houses. Some of the houses appear to have had fireplaces. But activities such as cooking and preparing food must have taken place out-of-doors. Archaeologists working at Statz found over 100 features, including earth ovens and shallow garbage pits, located *around* the houses. Only 2 features contained corn, so the people living there were probably not eating much corn.

## Mississippian Life

About AD 1000, life got more complicated in Wisconsin. We know that Woodland people lived here. Archaeologists think now that 2 very different groups *also* lived in Wisconsin at the same time. These were the Mississippians and the Oneota.

Archaeologists immediately recognized several differences between Woodland people and these new groups. The Mississippian and Oneota people used ground-up shell as temper in their pottery instead of grit or sand. The shapes and designs of their pottery were also very different from Woodland pottery. Mississippian and Oneota people also relied more on farming than did most Woodland people.

*This clam shell hoe was used at Aztalan. Where did the Mississippians find the shell?*

Mississippian sites appeared in Wisconsin about AD 1000. A huge site called **Cahokia** , (cuh **ho** kee a) located in present-day southern Illinois, was the center of Mississippian culture. Archaeologists estimate that up to 20,000 people may have lived there. That's a city the size of Stevens Point in Wisconsin today. To feed such large populations, the Mississippians had to be very good farmers. They grew corn and squash.

To control such large populations, Mississippian society had to have powerful leaders. Perhaps these leaders addressed crowds from the huge **platform mounds** and **plazas** that Mississippians constructed. Craftsmen and craftswomen made fine ornaments and shell-tempered pottery with interesting shapes and designs. So far, archaeologists have only found platform mounds at 2 sites in Wisconsin: at **Aztalan** (**Az** tuh lahn) and **Trempealeau** (**Trem** puh lo). Whatever it meant and whoever belonged to the culture, the Mississippian way of life did not last long in Wisconsin. Just 200 years later, those living at Aztalan and Trempealeau were gone. The sites were deserted.

Map by Amelia Janes, Earth Illustrated Inc.

Mississippian sites in Illinois and Wisconsin

**platform mounds:** Large earthen mound with a flat top    **plazas:** Open public areas

## Aztalan, a Mississippian Outpost?

Occupied between about AD 900 and 1200, Aztalan looked very different from other village sites of similar age in Wisconsin. The town was located next to the Crawfish River. Four tall walls made of wooden posts enclosed the town. Some archaeologists suggest that the walls were built for defense. Others suggest that the leaders at Aztalan used them to control who could go and who could stay.

*Mississipian platform at Aztalan*

**DID YOU KNOW?**

People started using bows and arrows sometime between AD 600 and 800. Late Woodland, Oneota, and Mississippians all used bows and made small triangular-shaped arrowheads. Before this time, people only used spears to hunt.

Within these walls, the people at Aztalan built 3 large platform mounds. A large natural low hill may have been used as a fourth mound. Archaeologists have found the remains of houses—both circular and rectangular in shape. They also found a plaza located between the mounds.

Different activities took place on the top of each of the mounds. One mound had a series of fire pits that were lined with white sand. This was probably where the town kept its **sacred** (**sa** crud) fires burning as part of a ceremony. People poured white sand into the fire pits to make them pure.

**sacred:** Deserving of respect

On top of one of the other mounds, the people at Aztalan had built a small structure. They placed 11 burials inside and then burned the building down. The third mound, capped with a layer of clay, contained pits where corn was stored.

Archaeologists are not sure who built Aztalan. Some suggest that people who came directly from Cahokia to set up a northern town with a local Woodland group. Other archaeologists suggest that Aztalan's founders came from close by. Perhaps the builders came from present-day northern Illinois and just took ideas from Cahokia. Perhaps local Woodland people who liked what the Mississippians were doing at Cahokia actually built Aztalan.

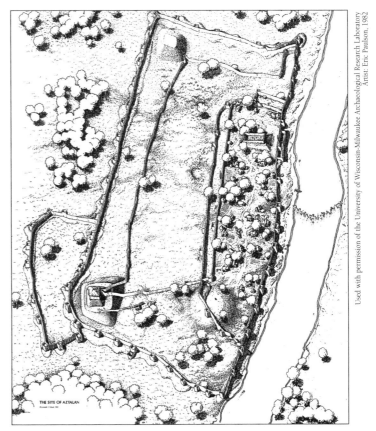

*Bird's-eye view of the Aztalan site*

Archaeologists are also uncertain about who lived at Aztalan because the pottery there is very different from pottery found in other nearby sites. Some of the pottery was clearly Mississippian. These pots were shell-tempered and had Mississippian shapes and designs. Other pottery was grit-tempered, like the pottery that Woodland people made. But this pottery was shaped like the pots that Mississippian people made!

Archaeologists are left wondering: did different people move in to Aztalan or did just their *ideas move*? What kinds of ideas or even ways of talking or dressing have moved into your life through your friends, books, or television? We learn and adopt new styles all the time!

Woodland          Mississippian

*Can you name at least 3 differences between these 2 pots?*

## The Oneota

The Oneota are the third group of people that lived in Wisconsin around AD 1000. Like the Mississippians, the Oneota were farmers and made shell-tempered pottery. But the Oneota did not build platform or effigy mounds. Large Oneota villages have been found around Green Bay, western Lake Winnebago, Grand River Marsh, Lake Koshkonong, and La Crosse. Archaeologists still wonder who the Oneota were.

Did they **migrate** into Wisconsin from more southern locations? Were they a local Woodland population that changed under the influence of Mississippians? Archaeologists look for ways to test these hypotheses.

*Oneota Communities (white area)*

50    **migrate:** Move from one part of a country to another

# The Tremaine Site, an Oneota Village

From about AD 1300 to 1650, the La Crosse area was home to many Oneota people. The Oneota enjoyed living in the rich environment provided by the Mississippi River Valley. They had good land for growing corn and rivers and swampy areas to fish. They found plenty of game in both the river valley and hill country. Archaeologists have discovered the remains of large villages throughout the La Crosse area. Archaeologists have even found the remains of Oneota agricultural fields buried under layers of dirt left behind by flooding rivers.

Six hundred years ago, a group of Oneota established a village a few miles east of the Mississippi. They located their village on a terrace overlooking Halfway Creek. The Oneota lived in **longhouses**, which were very large houses shaped like cigars. When people first started living at the Tremaine site, the houses they built were about 85 feet long and about 20 feet wide.

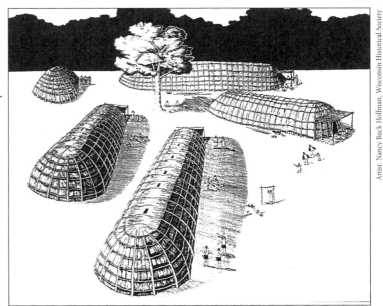

Oneota longhouses housed larger family groups.

## POSTHOLE PLAN

Here's an example of the way archaeologists use patterns of postholes to figure out what houses look like. This is a house at Aztalan.

Illustration Courtesy of the Wisconsin Archaeological Society

As the years passed, people rebuilt and made the houses even longer. They enlarged their houses to allow larger family groups to live together. Although about the same width, the later houses were almost double the length of the originals! One house was 165 feet long, about half the length of a football field! Archaeologists estimate that 15 to 30 people lived in the earlier houses. The later, larger houses held up to 60 people! Can you imagine how it would be to live in a house with 59 other people?

What did these houses look like after 600 years? Well, at first not much. Archaeologists discovered the houses by carefully excavating a large area and looking at the patterns of **postholes**. These postholes were what were left of the house's walls. Judging from the hundreds of small postholes, the walls of these longhouses were constructed of many, many poles. These walls were then probably covered with hides or branches and other brush. Inside the houses, there were hearths, storage pits for food, and burials.

The way that these features were found together in various parts of the houses suggests that a number of small family groups shared a longhouse.

Remember those small houses at the Statz site? The people at the Tremaine site must have lived very differently.

Archaeologists recovered animal bones and plant remains from storage and garbage pits inside and outside the longhouses. From their analyses of these remains, archaeologists know that the Oneota hunted deer, bison, elk, beaver, muskrat, black bear, passenger pigeon, duck, turkey, and turtle. They also fished for catfish, bullheads, drum, and even sturgeon.

Interestingly, the only type of bison bone found at this site were bison **scapulae** (**skap** yuh luh), or shoulder blades. The Oneota used these heavy bison scapulae as hoes to work in their fields. The plant remains included corn, wild rice, beans, nuts such as acorns and hickory, and seeds from blackberries, huckleberries, and blueberries. Sounds like the La Crosse area was nature's supermarket! This makes it all the more remarkable that the Oneota apparently left this area sometime in the late 1600s and moved west across the Mississippi River.

## Making a Bridge Between Early Indians and Indian Nations

It has been difficult for archaeologists to trace the ancestors of most American Indian Nations—such as the **Ho-Chunk**, **Menominee**, and **Ojibwe**—back to the earlier groups you just read about in this chapter. Current evidence suggests that the Woodland way of life lasted in *northern* Wisconsin until the arrival of the first Europeans in the 1600s.

But the Woodland tradition may have ended in *southern* Wisconsin 400 years earlier.

The Menominee may have their origins in Wisconsin's Woodland tradition. Some Oneota probably became the **Ioway** Nation. Some Oneota may have become the Ho-Chunk Nation.

There are several reasons why it is hard to trace the ancestors of today's Indian Nations. The arrival of Europeans in North America caused much change and confusion. Indian life in Wisconsin began to change even before Europeans actually set foot in Wisconsin and began to write down everything they saw.

As Europeans settled in the eastern part of North America, they pushed tribal people west. This movement west added new groups of Indian people to Wisconsin's landscape. And with them and increasing numbers of Europeans, came European diseases.

Many Indian people died. People from some Indian Nations now lived together with people from other Indian Nations.

Many Indian people also began to use more and more European goods. Once everyone starts using the same tools, it's hard for archaeologists to determine who lived in a particular village and left those tools behind.

Think of all of these changes—new people, villages where more than one group of Indian people lived at the same time, and many different groups of people using the same tools. That's why it's difficult for archaeologists to identify the specific ancestors of today's Indian Nations in Wisconsin.

# Looking Back

As the numbers of Indian people grew in Wisconsin, life changed. People started to stay longer in particular places. They began to farm, make pottery, and bury their dead in burial mounds. About a thousand years ago, 3 different groups—the Woodland, the Mississippian, and the Oneota—started living their lives in different ways. Some people focused more on farming, but others continued to hunt and gather most of their food. Different groups of people made different kinds of pottery, built different types of mounds, and lived in different kinds of villages.

# Chapter 5

# Stories in Stone:
# Looking at Wisconsin Rock Art

The only region in Wisconsin that remained untouched by glaciers is the southwestern part of the state, known as the **Driftless Area** . Here, steep cliffs of limestone and sandstone interrupt the prairie. No glacier smashed and smoothed the rough rock edges in this part of the state. The Driftless Area contains almost all of Wisconsin's caves and rock shelters. These provided excellent cold weather homes that protected many generations of Indian people who camped there. The rocky surfaces in and around more than one hundred rock shelters, overhangs, and caves also provided areas for people to produce rock art.

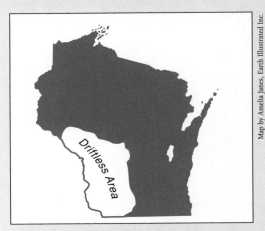

Map by Amelia Janes, Earth Illustrated Inc.

*Why is so much rock art in the Driftless Area ?*

56

## Think About It

What kinds of rock art are found in Wisconsin? Where can you find it? Do archaeologists know what stories the rock art tells?

# What Is Rock Art?

Rock art includes all images carved and painted on stone walls. Those that are carved are **petroglyphs** (**pet** ruh glifs). Those that are painted are **pictographs** (**pic** to grafs). These can provide important clues to the lifeways and beliefs of those who lived in Wisconsin long ago. But we don't know now, and we may never know, the artists' exact message. Do their drawings tell something about the beliefs of those who painted or carved them? Do they relate to the stories that they told to each other and passed down to their children and their children's children? These stories formed part of their **oral tradition**, the history and tales that people told to one another. Wisconsin's ancient Indian populations did not write their stories with words.

# Ancient Images at the Gottschall Site

Archaeologist Robert J. Salzer has found exciting clues to one rock art puzzle in his work at the Gottschall site in northwestern Iowa County. His research team found evidence indicating that Indians conducted ceremonies there. The archaeologists discovered more than 40 images painted on the wall and ceiling. These paintings relate directly to ceremonies and stories that still belong to the Ho-Chunk and other Indian nations. Remember that it's easier for archaeologists to discover how people lived and what they ate rather than what they believed, taught, or thought about. That's why the clues of the Gottschall site are so important. Dr. Salzer hypothesizes that the rock art and other discoveries at the site show that the artists were distant ancestors of the Ho-Chunk. The Ho-Chunk have successfully handed down these traditions and stories for many, many generations.

## Meeting Red Horn

In 1984, Dr. Salzer and crews of archaeologists and volunteers began spending summers at the Gottschall rock shelter. They documented the rock art and excavated through the layers of dirt on the rock shelter floor. How did archaeologists find out about the site? Several years earlier, some kids were playing at the rock shelter. One of the kids who was using a flashlight shone it on a wall and, amazingly, discovered images that had been painted there long ago. In 1992, Dr. Salzer and his crew even found a 10-inch high sculpture of a human head!

Map by Amelia Janes, Earth Illustrated Inc.

Gottschall
Site

*This is the sculpture of the human head found at the Gottschall site.*

*Archaeologists at the Gottschall site rock shelter needed extra light to excavate.*

Dr. Salzer believes that the paintings show figures from the legend of Red Horn, a kind of superhero in the oldest stories of the Ho-Chunk and Ioway Nations. Sometimes Red Horn was known as "He-who-wears-human-heads-as-earrings." This superhero of long ago had many adventures. The sculpture of the head probably represents a specific character in the Red Horn legend.

As the youngest of 10 brothers, Red Horn first showed his supernatural powers when he won a footrace and revealed that he had red hair. Later he became a leader of his nation and a hero to his people. He had several special friends who helped him protect his people from a group of giants trying to destroy them. These friends included Turtle and Thunderbird, a creature who is also known as "Storms-as-he walks." One of the giants, a red-haired **chieftainess** (**cheef** tuh ness) also befriended Red Horn. Red Horn and the chieftainess defeated the other giants in a series of challenges: a ball game, a shooting match, a dice game, and a breath-holding contest. Red Horn then married the red-haired chieftainess.

*The straight lines surrounding the image are cut marks made by a saw! People were actually trying to remove the rock art from the wall. Fortunately, they could not break the image away. Since this attempt, the state passed a law in 1996 to protect rock art sites.*

*Red Horn*

**chieftainess:** Woman chief

But the trials against the evil giants were not quite over. In the final contest, the giants out-wrestled Red Horn and his friends and killed them. Red Horn's sons finally defeated the giants and brought Red Horn, Storms-as-he-walks, and Turtle back to life. Then these 3 superheroes continued their adventures. Because people enjoyed hearing about Red Horn, storytellers have kept the legend alive for hundreds of years. Along with the rock artists, they have given us another clue to understand part of Wisconsin's past.

## Looking at Red Horn

Of the many pictographs at the Gottschall rock shelter, one large group contains both humans and animals, including Turtle and Thunderbird. The large human figures might be the giants in the Red Horn legend. The one painted with red hair is likely to be Red Horn's wife.

Tracing by Mary Steinhauer

*Red Horn Group*

The smaller figure near the falcon-like Thunderbird might be Red Horn himself. Did you notice the lower right corner where a small man holds a long pipe? His message may be that this pictograph carries special meaning, because pipes are sacred to most North American Indian cultures.

# "Attacking Giants Are Met in Contest; Ball-stick Game Goes Against Giants Who Are Killed"

We edited a version of a longer tale, originally written by Sam Blowsnake, and included as part of "The Red Horn Cycle," in Paul Radin's *Winnebago Hero Cycles: A Study in Aboriginal Literature*, published by Indiana University.

In the morning they [Red Horn (He-who-wears-human-heads-as-earrings) and his friends, including Turtle, Kunu, Thunderbird (Storms-as-he-walks), Otter and Marten] went to encounter the giants. The one who was helping the giants most was a giantess with red hair, just like Red Horn's hair.

Then said Turtle to Wolf, "My friend, let us go and match the ball-sticks." This they did, placing Red Horn's ball-stick together with that of the giantess so that he might play against her. "When shall we be ready to play ball? I am getting rather anxious," [she said]. To which Turtle replied, "Just as soon as my friend comes we shall start." Then the chieftainess said, "Who is your friend that it takes him so long to come?" "Wait til he comes! You certainly will laugh when you see him." "Why, what is there funny about him that I should laugh?" said the giantess. "Just wait till he comes," said Turtle, "just wait till he comes, and then you will see."

Soon after that [Red Horn] came and Turtle said to him, "My friend, let us go over there and look at the sticks of the ball players." They went and found the giantess there and, when she saw him, she most certainly laughed and bowed her head. "There you are," said Turtle. "I thought you said you would not laugh?" "Yes," said the giantess, "but I did not laugh at him." "Well," said Turtle, "Look at him again." The giantess looked again and the small heads he was wearing in his ears stuck their tongues out at her. Again she laughed and bowed her head. Then said Turtle to He-who-wears-human-heads-as-earrings [Red Horn], "My friend, let us, you and I, start the game." So they tossed the ball to the giants.

When it came near the ground, Red Horn stuck his stick out keeping the others away from Turtle. Turtle caught the ball. Then he ran among the giants swinging his stick. He said, "Stand back or I will knock some of you down!" The giants' sticks rattled about him but he came out with the ball. Turtle then got the ball again and sent it through the goal into the very midst of the giants. Thus they won the first point. Turtle shouted, "Come on! Come on! It is such fun to play ball!"

Again they played. The ball was tossed up and again Turtle got the ball and whirled it in the midst of the giants. Getting clear, he threw the ball just beyond the place where Otter and Marten were standing. Then Otter put the ball through the goal.

The game was started again. Storms-as-he-walks and the giant chieftainess were together at the goal as before. Turtle caught the ball and whirled it into the midst of the giants. When he got clear he threw the ball low and let it rise as it went farther and farther. Just where the giantess and Storms-as-he-walks stood, there it lit. Storms-as-he-walks got the ball and ran with it, the chieftainess after him. When she caught up with him, he ran harder and caused it to thunder. The chieftainess got frightened and jumped aside. Storms-as-he-walks ran through the goal, winning another point. "Come on! Come on! It is such fun to play ball! Let us start again."

Kunu and Turtle were at the throwing-off place. Turtle said, "My friend usually swings his stick pretty wide." And sure enough Kunu swung his stick in such a way as to interfere with the giant's stick, giving Turtle a chance to catch the ball. Getting clear of the giants, Turtle threw the ball to the place where Red Horn and the giantess were standing. Red Horn got the ball and ran with it just as she [the giantess] caught up to Red Horn, [he] turned about and the little faces in his ears stuck out their tongues at her and the eyes winked at her. When she saw the faces, she laughed and let down her stick. And so Red Horn ran through the goal, winning the point. The giants were thus beaten in all four points. The giant chieftainess lost the game on account of her falling in love with Red Horn.

## Looking Back

Rock art provides an amazing window into the past. The ancient images, sometimes painted, sometimes pecked into rock surfaces, give us clues about what people were doing, thinking, and feeling. Many rock art sites have been found in southwestern Wisconsin amid the rocky outcrops of the Driftless Area. The Gottschall site is one of the most outstanding, because it has such a complete story of Red Horn, a story told by generations and generations of the Ho-Chunk people.

# Chapter 6

## Furs and Forts

◆ ◆ ◆

WHS Archives, CF 5587

*Great Lakes Indians invented birchbark canoes. The first Europeans traveled to Wisconsin in Indian-made canoes.*

The first Europeans to arrive in Wisconsin were the French. It would be easy to say that everything changed when these first explorers arrived in 1634. But it didn't. Life had begun to change for some Indians in Wisconsin even before the French actually set foot in the Midwest!

How did the Europeans affect life in Wisconsin before they actually arrived in the region? Some Wisconsin Indians received European trade goods and probably European diseases through their trade with other tribes who *were already* in contact with the newcomers.

## Think About It

Who were the first Europeans in Wisconsin? Which Indian peoples were already here? Why did Europeans come to Wisconsin? How did Indian lives change?

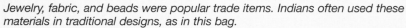

*Jewelry, fabric, and beads were popular trade items. Indians often used these materials in traditional designs, as in this bag.*

## Adapting to New People

At first, Indian villages and campsites looked much like they did before the arrival of Europeans and their trade goods. Most Indians kept making pottery and stone tools the way they had always done. But within a few generations, people were no longer following some of these old ways. Instead, they chose to trade for and use some European goods. Brass pots and metal knives worked better than breakable clay pots and easily dulled stone knives.

Indians, however, did not accept European ways entirely. Indian groups adopted some objects that made life easier, like knives and pots and cloth. But they also continued to use traditional materials. Native people still used birchbark to make some types of containers and canoes. They still used bone to make fishing lures. Most Native people also continued to follow their own ways of life—hunting, fishing, gathering, and gardening—as their territories and as the seasons allowed.

But for some Indians, daily activities *did* change as they became more involved with the fur trade. Europeans wanted many furs. So Indians were no longer trapping just a few animals to provide for their own families. Instead, they were spending many hours a day hunting, trapping, and preparing furs for the European market. All of this new work took time away from other activities like tending crops, fishing, and gathering wild rice. Once all or most of the fur-bearing animals were gone from an area, hunters had to travel greater distances or move their villages more frequently to find more animals.

## Wisconsin, Home to Many

When Europeans arrived in Wisconsin in the early 1600s, many different Indian Nations lived in the area. Wisconsin was probably the homeland for several of these groups, like the Menominee, Ho-Chunk, and **Santee Dakota** . But a number of other Native peoples now lived in Wisconsin who had been forced to move from their own traditional homelands farther to the east and north and south.

These Native groups included the

- Ojibwe,
- **Potawatomi** (Poh tah **wah** tuh mee),
- **Huron** (Hyuh rahn),
- **Petun** (Peh **tune**),
- **Ottawa** (Aw tah wah),
- **Kickapoo** ,
- **Sauk** ,
- **Mesquakie (Fox)** (Mes **kwah** kee),
- **Mascouten** (Mas **ku** tun),
- Ioway, and
- **Miami** .

Unfortunately, archaeologists have found it hard to identify where particular groups lived. Can you think why?

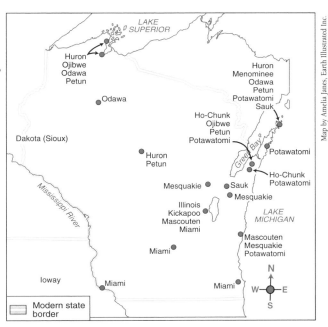

Map by Amelia Janes, Earth Illustrated Inc.

*Indian Communities in 1600*

69

Remember, archaeologists work with the objects that people leave behind. Once most Indian people began using the same kinds of European artifacts, it is difficult, or nearly impossible, to tell whether the Potawatomi or Menominee may have occupied a village. That's the reason archaeologists need historic records or oral tradition to place a particular group in a specific location.

And just think of the problems future archaeologists may have! How will they identify different groups of people based on material objects when *everybody* is using and wearing the same things? People from Alaska to Zimbabwe are wearing Nikes. Future archaeologists can only hope that different groups of people will keep using some of their own local stuff!

## The French Fur Trade

The first Europeans who arrived in Wisconsin showed no interest in building permanent homes and farms. They only wanted to trade their goods for furs. The French, followed by the British, wanted as many furs as possible to ship back to the markets in Europe. That's why the earliest European sites in Wisconsin were only small forts and trading posts.

The men in these forts and trading posts worked to make the trade grow with the various Indian Nations. In the late 1600s, the French built several small forts along Lake Superior, Green Bay, and the Mississippi River. Archaeologists have searched for these early French sites. But few have been found.

The French basically controlled the fur trade in Wisconsin for the 90 years between 1670 and 1760. During this period, contact between Europeans and the various Indian Nations in Wisconsin increased. So, it's not surprising that for this time period archaeologists have found greater amounts and a greater variety of trade goods at Indian village sites. They found iron knives, brass pots, bottle fragments, gun parts, and many different types of trade beads.

Archaeologists also found **Jesuits** (**jez** yu it) rings and medals. The Jesuits were priests who were **missionaries** (**mih** shun air eez), people who hoped to convince Indians to give up their own religions and join the Catholic Church.

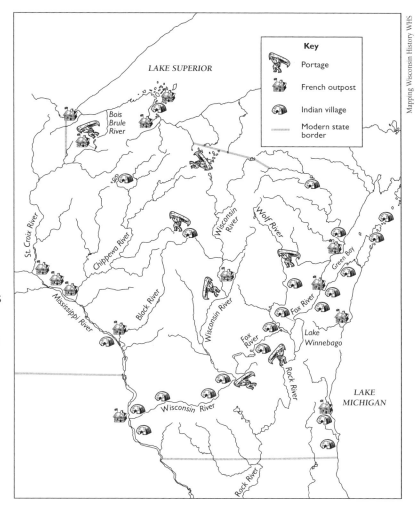

Mapping Wisconsin History WHS

**Key**
Portage
French outpost
Indian village
Modern state border

LAKE SUPERIOR

Bois Brule River

St. Croix River

Chippewa River

Mississippi River

Black River

Wisconsin River

Wolf River

Green Bay

Fox River

Lake Winnebago

Fox River

Rock River

Wisconsin River

Rock River

LAKE MICHIGAN

*Fur Trade and Exploration*

# Growing Conflicts

The French got along well with some Indian Nations but did not get along with others, like the Mesquakie. There were many reasons for the dislike and distrust between these groups. First, the Mesquakie could not forget that in the years 1711–1712, the French refused to help them when their people were being attacked by Ottawa and Huron-Petuns.

Second, the Mesquakie did not want the French to trade with some other Native groups, like the Dakota. The Dakota lived to the west in what is now Minnesota. But once the Mesquakie moved to the Fox River (in about 1680) they were in a good position to try to break up French trade with people to the west.

*Europeans traded knives such as these for Indian furs.*

*Earrings of German silver were popular fur trade items.*

*This beaded powder horn held gun powder, an item that Europeans brought to Wisconsin. Europeans also brought the beads that Indians worked into designs on the strap.*

# WHY WAS THE FOX RIVER IMPORTANT FOR FUR TRADE?

The Fox River was a very important link between eastern and western fur trade markets. The river provided an easy route between Lake Michigan and the Mississippi River through a **portage** (**por** tuj) to the Wisconsin River. The Fox River flows to Lake Michigan, and the Wisconsin River flows into the Mississippi River.

In south-central Wisconsin, the Fox River flows close to the Wisconsin River. These rivers are only about a mile and a half apart at what is today the city of Portage. But these 2 rivers flow in completely different directions, and their waters end up thousands of miles apart!

By carrying a canoe the short distance across the portage between the Fox and Wisconsin Rivers, a traveler or trader could go from the Great Lakes (and as far east as the Atlantic Ocean) all the way to the Mississippi River and then down to the Gulf of Mexico. No other state offered such a good river route from the Great Lakes to the Mississippi River.

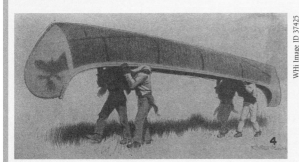

WHi Image ID 37425

*Carrying a canoe across a portage*

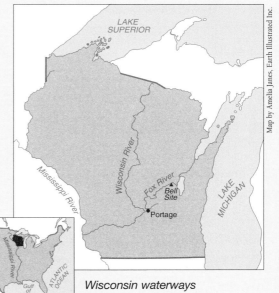

Map by Amelia Janes, Earth Illustrated Inc.

*Wisconsin waterways*

**portage:** A place where people had to carry their canoes over land

In the early 1700s the French began a war against the Mesquakie Nation. The French hoped to destroy the Mesquakie. Did you ever think that Wisconsin could be the site of a naval **bombardment** (**bahm** bard munt)? In 1716 French gunboats bombarded a stockaded Mesquakie village. Archaeologists found this village, known now as the Bell site. This village was located on the southern shore of **Lake Buttes des Morts** (**bew duh more**) in present day Winnebago County. There archaeologists found what was left of a stockade. They also found small bomb fragments, which were shot from guns aboard the French boats.

In this particular investigation, the archaeologists were lucky. Written records and archaeological excavations definitely helped them positively to identify an early Mesquakie village. Between 1680 and 1730, when the Mesquakie lived there, they were still making their own pottery and many of their own tools. Finding this village helped archaeologists identify other early Mesquakie sites.

## The British Arrive

In 1760, the French lost a war to the British. They fought most of this war in Europe. But they also fought in North America. Historians call the North American part of the war the French and Indian War. Many of the Indian Nations in Wisconsin fought for the French. That's because the French were their main trading partners.

But the French lost. So the British gained control of the Wisconsin fur trade. Trade goods found at Indian sites dating to

WHi (X3) 50883

*Jewelry, such as this silver pin, was often traded for furs.*

**bombardment:** Huge attack with bombs

this time reflect this change. For example, after 1760, silver artifacts produced by Canadian, English, and American silversmiths became very popular. Archaeologists found these silver artifacts at many Indian sites.

Around this time, most Indians also stopped making many of their traditional goods. They stopped making pottery out of clay. Few if any Native people were still making stone tools. This means that archaeologists have a much harder time trying to recognize specific Indian groups based solely on the goods they made.

Wisconsin was under British rule from 1760 until the end of the American Revolution in 1783. During the revolution, Wisconsin remained under British control. And the fur trade between the British and Indians continued to thrive. Most Indian tribes in Wisconsin now supported the British. After all, the British were now their trading partners. So once again, the Indians found themselves on the losing side.

When the British lost the war, Wisconsin became part of the new American government. But the British stayed in Wisconsin and controlled trade with the Indians there until 1812. That year, the British and Americans went to war again. In 1815, at the end of that war, the Americans were now ready to take control of Wisconsin. That's when the lives of many Indians began to change even more rapidly than they had under the French and British.

## Rock Island, Gateway to Wisconsin

Hundreds of years ago, many travelers' first view of Wisconsin was Rock Island. Rock Island was a stopping-off point for people making their way from upper Michigan down to the Door **Peninsula** (peh **nin** su lah).

peninsula: A piece of land that sticks out from a larger mass and is almost completely surrounded by water

Between 1640 and the late 1700s, many Native groups were on the move. Back east, increasing numbers of Europeans and the powerful **Iroquois** (**ear** uh coy or **ear** uh quah) Nation were disrupting the lives of many Native people. Some of these people (including the Potawatomi, Huron, Petun, and Ottawa) came to Rock Island. But no written records document the way most of these people lived on Rock Island.

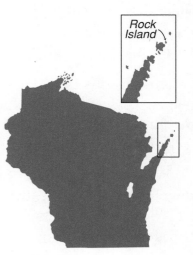

Map by Amelia Janes, Earth Illustrated Inc.

Rock Island

Fortunately, archaeologists excavating in 1969 and the early 1970s discovered **stratified** (**strat** ih fyd) artifacts and features. Archaeologists used this information to figure out what these different groups did more than 200 years ago.

Artist: Phoebe Heklo

*Bell Site II pottery*

First, a small group of Potawatomi stopped at Rock Island in the 1640s. They left behind a small amount of a distinctive pottery (called Bell Site Type II), stone tools, and a few French trade goods.

Second, less than 10 years later, more Indians arrived. They were the Huron, Petun, and Ottawa. All of these groups were trying to get away from the Iroquois! The archaeologists found pottery known **Huron-Incised** (in **sised**) at the site. Archaeologists knew that the

Artist: Phoebe Heklo

*Huron-Incised pottery. Incised lines are those carved into the pot.*

**stratified:** Layered

Huron-Petun-Ottawa combined Nation made this kind of pottery. So archaeologists realized that the Huron, Petun, and Ottawa people had lived on Rock Island.

Archaeologists also found tools made of bone and stone, including a tool made from a bear jaw. They discovered seeds of corn, beans, and squash. They also found trade goods, such as glass beads and the tip of a huge iron knife.

The archaeologists found features as well. They uncovered and mapped evidence of a number of ditches and postholes. The patterns of these postholes and ditches suggest that the Huron-Petun-Ottawa had built a 5-sided stockade to defend themselves. They probably feared being attacked by the Iroquois.

A third Native group arrived in the 1670s. For the next 60 years, Rock Island again became home to a group of Potawatomi. The many artifacts and features suggest that the Potawatomi apparently stayed for several generations. Interestingly, they left behind some Bell Site Type II pottery. They were still making and using the same kind of pottery found in their earlier village!

Then, a fourth group arrived. For a brief time in the late 1670s, a few Frenchmen joined the Potawatomi. The artifacts from both the French and the Potawatomi survived. Archaeologists found thousands of artifacts brought by the French: glass beads, shell beads, brass pots, iron axes, Jesuit rings and knives, and **gunflints** .

**gunflints:** Stones used to make a spark to fire old-style guns

## DID YOU KNOW?

To fire a gun hundreds of years ago, you pulled the trigger, and a piece of fine-grained rock, a gunflint, struck against a piece of metal. The resulting spark ignited some black powder. This mini-explosion pushed the bullet through the gun's barrel and through the air. Archaeologists can examine the shape and color of gunflints to see if they were made here, or imported from England or France.

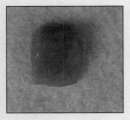

*Gunflint*

At Rock Island, archaeologists found plenty of Indian-made artifacts made from bone and **catlinite** (**cat** luh nite). Archaeologists also found a number of tools made from the lower jaws of bears and **harpoons**, barbed spears made from bone or antler to catch fish. During these years, more and more Potawatomi also decided to make arrowheads out of metal brought by Europeans. The Potawatomi had adapted new materials to continue their own hunting traditions.

WHS Museum Collection

*This catlinite pipe bowl was a gift to James Duane Doty, a well-known leader in Wisconsin in the 1800s.*

**catlinite:** Red pipestone found in southern Minnesota

The Frenchmen on Rock Island built 2 small buildings. These buildings were separated from the Potawatomi village by a small stockade. One of the buildings had a rock-outlined fireplace. That's where these traders probably lived. The archaeologists concluded that the traders built this building with cedar planks that had been stuck upright in a ditch. It would not have looked anything like the kind of log cabin you often see pictured in storybooks or on maple syrup containers!

Why do you think archaeologists believe the traders used the second building just for storage? This building had no fireplace, and it would have been very difficult to live on Rock Island during winters without a source of warmth.

After the Potawatomi left, about 20 years passed, and then a fifth group arrived. These were Ottawa people who lived on Rock Island about 10 years between 1760 and 1770. The Ottawa continued to make and use some stone and bone tools, like harpoons and a few arrowheads. But they had essentially stopped making their own pottery.

Archaeologists hypothesize that these Ottawa rarely made pottery because they were too busy preparing furs for trade. By this time, it was also easier to trade furs for brass pots.

This Ottawa "layer" of the site held many more brass pots than were found in the older villages. Archaeologists discovered only a few Ottawa arrowheads made of stone, and these were the smallest and lightest of any found on the island. Perhaps this means the Ottawa no longer valued stone weapons because they had new materials for hunting.

For hundreds of years, Rock Island provided a home to many people. During these years, the world changed greatly. By examining the artifacts left behind on this island, archaeologists have been able to document some of the changes that took place. Archaeologists have discovered the way people adapted to the changes in their lives.

Now, Rock Island is a state park, and campers and picnickers may well be leaving behind traces of our early twenty-first century life . . . By the way, where did you put that Frisbee? Did you leave behind your Packers cap?

## Looking Back

The French were the first Europeans to enter Wisconsin. At that time in the 1600s, Wisconsin was home to many Indian Nations. These included the Ho-Chunk, Menominee, Ojibwe, Potawatomi, Mesquakie, Dakota, Huron, and Miami. At first the Europeans just wanted to trade for furs. They were not interested in farming or building permanent cities and towns. But the fur trade forever changed the way Indian groups were living.

Indian lives began to change as many people spent more time hunting and preparing furs for the fur trade. Indian Nations also began to abandon old traditions such as making pottery and stone tools. They began to use more and more European-made goods, such as brass pots for cooking and metal knives for hunting.

# Chapter 7

# Mines, Timber, and Farms

◆ ◆ ◆

At the beginning of the 1800s, American Indian Nations controlled almost all of the land within Wisconsin's present borders. The only exceptions were European settlements at places like Green Bay and Prairie du Chien. By the end of the 1830s, however, **treaties** between Indian Nations and the U.S. government completely changed that picture. Now much of the land within Wisconsin had become the property of the U.S. government.

The U.S. government offered this land for sale to people moving into Wisconsin. This land soon provided homes to many different peoples moving from across the United States and other parts of the world. Eleven American Indian Nations—6 bands of Ojibwe,

WHi (W6) 23848

*In southwest Wisconsin, you can still see lead-mining pits dug over 100 years ago!*

82    **treaties:** Official written agreement between nations

the Menominee, Ho-Chunk, Potawatomi, **Oneida** , (O **ni** duh) and
**Stockbridge-Munsee** —now shared Wisconsin with New England Yankees,
southerners, Germans, African Americans, Swedes, Norwegians, Italians, Belgians,
Czechs, Irish, Welsh, French, English, Swiss, and Cornish . . . to name just a few!
The new people came looking for new lives in the lead mines of southwestern
Wisconsin, in the deep forests of the north, and on the rich—and sometimes not so
rich—farmlands across the state.

## Think About It

In the 1800s, how many Indian Nations remained in Wisconsin? What other
people were now living here? How did these new arrivals make a living?

## Mining in the Driftless Area

In the early 1800s, large numbers of settlers came to southwestern Wisconsin for one purpose: to make money by mining **galena** (guh **lee** nuh). The settlers then melted the galena in hot furnaces to produce lead. This soft metal had many important uses in the 1800s, including being made into **lead shot**.

Indian groups had mined and used galena from this region since the Archaic period. After the Europeans arrived, the Mesquakie, Sauk, and Ho-Chunk began to mine a lot more. These Native groups now used the galena for trade, lead shot, and to make other objects for themselves.

Most of the new miners came from the southern and northeastern United States and from the British Isles (England, Scotland and Ireland). In their search for galena, the settlers dug thousands and thousands of pits across the landscape of southwestern Wisconsin. The men spent so much time underground that they earned the nickname "badgers"! Where have you heard that name before? You can still see many of these pits today. Some are only a few feet deep and wide, but others are 20 feet deep and 20 feet wide!

At first, most miners only stayed at their **diggings** during the summer months. They returned to more settled areas, like the town of Galena in Illinois, during the

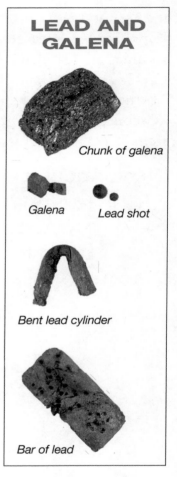

**LEAD AND GALENA**

*Chunk of galena*

*Galena*    *Lead shot*

*Bent lead cylinder*

*Bar of lead*

84    **galena:** A shiny gray mineral used to make lead    **lead shot:** Round bullets    **diggings:** Mine sites

winter. But gradually they excavated more and more galena. Then people built **smelters** near these mines.

These miners needed to eat, of course, and so they and other people who moved into the area started to farm. Then merchants arrived to build stores. More and more miners began to stay all year round. Soon small communities appeared throughout southwestern Wisconsin. And towns sprang up, like Potosi, New Diggings, Mineral Point, and the forgotten Hardscrabble.

## Hardscrabble, Grant County: Newcomers to an Old Land

Hardscrabble, founded in 1824 near the present-day town of Hazel Green, was one of the first *permanent* Euro-American settlements in Wisconsin's lead region. But Hardscrabble was abandoned. Its location was forgotten until it was accidently rediscovered during a 1980s construction project. That's when archaeologists discovered a foundation for a stone building (with a dirt floor) and hundreds of artifacts dating to the early 1800s. They found fragments of plates made in England, handblown (instead of machine-made) bottle glass, silverware, clay pipes, musket balls, as well as miners' tools like picks and shovels, cubes of galena, and animal bones from past meals. The archaeologists even found an 1823 silver dollar from Mexico. That may seem strange, but until the 1840s, people in the Midwest used foreign money because of a shortage of U.S. coins.

Map by Amelia Janes, Earth Illustrated Inc.

Hardscrabble

**smelters:** Large ovens to melt and process lead

85

Two of the more interesting discoveries that archaeologists made were portions of a high-laced shoe and a fragment of a cup with a nursery rhyme. These artifacts suggest that women and children had lived in Hardscrabble. Such an idea **contradicts** (cahn truh **dix**) some people's view that only men lived in the earliest mining towns.

We would like to ask other questions about life in these early mining towns but, unfortunately, we may never find the answers at Hardscrabble. The rest of this site was destroyed before archaeologists could investigate.

*High-laced shoe*

## Logging in the Northern Woods

In the mid-1800s, opportunities to work in Wisconsin's northern woods attracted people already living in the state, like the local Ojibwe. The woods also attracted others from around the world, particularly from countries in Northern Europe, like Norway. At this time in our country's history, wood was the most common material used in construction. People needed huge amounts to build homes and factories. There was no electricity yet, so people also needed wood to fuel the fires that powered the steamboats and locomotives. At that time, gas and electric-powered motors had not yet been invented.

During the next 100 years, loggers cut down millions of trees and shipped them to points east, south, and west. The people who worked in the logging industry built many towns, sawmills, camps, dams, and railroad tracks. But after they cleared the forests of usable trees, people abandoned most of these sites. The sites were left to rot and crumble, and eventually vegetation covered them over.

**contradicts:** Is the opposite of

In the beginning, loggers depended upon rivers and streams to float the cut logs downstream, out of the woods, and down to settlements with sawmills. First, they cut trees during the winter. Next they hauled the cut trees over roads that had been deliberately covered with ice. The ice made for smoother, easier hauling. Then the loggers piled the cut trees next to lakes and rivers. The loggers selected pine trees to cut because pine would float. Other kinds of trees were too heavy and sank.

As soon as the lake and river ice thawed in the spring, the log "drive" began. Skilled workers rode the logs downstream to the mills, using **pike poles** and **peaveys** to control the logs as they floated. A pike pole was about 16 feet long with a metal point on one end. A peavey was a 5 foot pole with a metal point on one end and a hook on the side.

WHi (X3) 30662

*Rolling logs into the river*

In the late 1800s, logging technology was beginning to change. Transporting logs by railroad became more popular. Because they no longer depended on the rivers, loggers could work year round. Now they also could cut hardwood trees, like oak, basswood, and maple.

The location of lumber camps also changed. Camps no longer had to be located next to water, so loggers built camps deeper and deeper into the woods. The loggers also used new, more efficient tools. Until around 1880, loggers used axes to cut the trees. But after this time, pairs of workers used large crosscut saws (6 to 7 feet long) to cut down the trees.

87

Early camps were fairly small and located next to water. A few loggers cooked, ate, and slept in a single log cabin, about 30 feet long and 20 feet wide. To keep these cabins warmer, workers often piled up dirt against the foundations of the cabins as **insulation** (in suh **la** shun), trapping the heat inside the cabin.

By the late 1800s, the logging camps were much larger. Loggers lived in **dingle-style** buildings. These buildings consisted of a bunkhouse, about 65 feet long and 30 feet wide, connected by a covered passageway to a large kitchen or dining hall. These dingle-style buildings could house between 50 and 100 workers. Large logging camps also had separate buildings for stores, blacksmiths, and carpentry shops. In the newer camps that transported logs by railroad, the camp's planners laid out buildings in straight lines facing the tracks.

Although diaries and logging company records provide some information about life in these logging camps and towns, much is missing or was never written down. Archaeologists look to the ground to find additional clues about the ways these loggers lived.

*Loggers in front of dingle-style building*

# The Sherry and Gerry Logging Camp, Oconto County

The U.S. Forest Service owns many acres of woods in northern Wisconsin. And these woods contain the **remnants** of hundreds of logging camps. To better understand these sites and their impact on the forest, archaeologists have been locating, mapping, and sometimes excavating these logging camps.

Sherry and Gerry Logging Camp

In 1990, archaeologists mapped and then excavated portions of a small logging camp located on a **tributary** (**trih** byu teh ree) to the Oconto River, in western Oconto County. They documented the remnants of 5 buildings. There were no standing walls, of course—only 5 rectangular low spots in the ground surrounded by the low dirt hills that the loggers had once piled up next to the walls for insulation. Who had lived there and when?

Historic records show that between 1876 and 1878, Henry Sherry and George Gerry, owned and operated a logging camp in this *general* area. Unfortunately, these records do not provide an exact location. Were these 5 buildings the Sherry and Gerry camp? Based on the artifacts at the site, the archaeologists believe so. None of the artifacts or features they found definitely dates to either earlier than 1876 or later than 1878, the years the camp operated.

**remnants:** Things that are left  **tributary:** A small stream that flows into a larger waterway

89

Archaeologists found some of these artifacts, like fragments of peaveys, axes, and a few crosscut saws, just lying on the ground. They also excavated test units inside each of the building's foundations in order to figure out the way people had used the buildings. Based on the buildings' sizes and the artifacts that they found, the archaeologists identified a bunkhouse, a kitchen or dining hall (dingle style), and a hut for oxen.

*Lumber men using crosscut saw*

Archaeologists also hypothesize that the other 2 smaller buildings served as a cook's cabin and possibly a foreman's cabin. Archaeologists found a large storage pit inside that foreman's cabin. They think that the foreman may have used this pit to hide valuables. Within this building they also found a fragment of a rubber shoe marked with a New Brunswick shoemaker's mark. George Gerry, one of the possible owners of this camp, was born in New Brunswick, Canada, and he reportedly spent a lot of time in his logging camps. Do you think that the evidence of the marked shoe is merely a coincidence? Or would you hypothesize that George Gerry was actually there?

# Farms Across Wisconsin
# (Or You Can't Eat Lead and Pine Trees)

Everybody needs to eat, and many of the early settlers who came to mine and cut trees also farmed part of the year or belonged to families that did. Little by little, agriculture completely changed the landscape of most of Wisconsin, particularly in the southern half of the state.

Many Wisconsin farmers first planted wheat because it required little work during the growing season. But as the price of wheat fell and the soil lost the minerals necessary to grow it, farmers began to grow a variety of other crops, including corn and potatoes. Farmers also grew specialty crops like cranberries and cherries. They raised sheep, cattle, hogs, and poultry too.

Dairy farming, Wisconsin's most famous way of life, only became popular in the late 1880s after the invention of the round or **cylindrical** (sih **lin** drih kuhl) silo. Silos provided a good place to store food for the cows. Being able to store food

Farm silos

in silos meant that farmers could feed and milk their cows through the long cold winters. Only when farmers could maintain the cattle though winter could they seriously consider dairying. By the early 1900s, dairy cows could be found on over 90% of Wisconsin farms.

**DID YOU KNOW?**

Corn and potatoes were first cultivated by Indians in the Americas. Indians had been growing these crops for thousands of years before Europeans came to the Americas.

91

Many, many different people came to Wisconsin in the 1800s to establish farms. And through the beginning of the twentieth century, most people in Wisconsin were farmers. Farms were everywhere! Even today, thousands of farms dot Wisconsin's countryside. Were all these farms similar? Were Finnish farms in northern Wisconsin different from German farms in southern Wisconsin or from the African-American farms in Cheyenne Valley in western Wisconsin? You betcha! People built the kind of barns their families built "back home," wherever "home" was.

*A dairy farm in the 19th century*

Today, many family farms have been abandoned, have fallen into ruin, or have become homes for people who commute to their jobs in cities and towns. Most Wisconsin people today no longer farm and know nothing about this way of life. Archaeologists are interested in describing and explaining past human behavior, whether it happened 50 years ago or 12,000 years ago. Archaeologists hope that the patterns of artifacts and features left behind at Wisconsin's farmstead sites will provide much information about family farm lives. This information is not the kind that's recorded in history books or in people's personal letters, diaries, or memories.

## The 2 Pits Site: Farming Up North in Douglas County

The 2 Pits site is located in the Pine Barrens of northwestern Wisconsin. This particular part of the state never had many trees, and by the 1890s loggers had cut and hauled most of them away. Then fires swept through and burned the brush and stumps left behind. Many things—including poor soils, harsh climate, and distance from markets—made the Pine Barrens a difficult place to earn a living, particularly for farmers. Yet, in the 1890s businesses and local and state governments actively encouraged people to settle and farm there. Most of these farms struggled. Many failed.

Before archaeologists began their research, little was known about the 2 Pits site. Historic records suggest that people lived there for only about 30 years in the late 1800s and early 1900s. But no one knew anything about them.

Archaeologists found the remnants of 2 buildings (consisting of only low earthen hills, marking where the walls had once stood), a well, a garbage pit, and a number of other pits dug into the ground. They also documented a narrow ditch about a half foot deep and one to 2 feet wide that encircled the entire site. This trench probably was meant to serve as a

*Pine Barrens in northwestern Wisconsin*

**firebreak** . Farmers hoped to stop any fires from reaching the house. They often removed trees, bushes, fallen leaves, and other things that could easily catch fire from an area around the homestead to protect their homes and families.

**firebreak:** An area cleared of grass, shrubs, or trees in order to stop fires

In their test excavations, the archaeologists found a variety of household objects, including broken plates, stoneware jars, bottles, a few tin cans, a **snuff** jar, hand-made tools, clothing fasteners, and eating utensils. You may be surprised to know how much information that these little things reveal. The bottles were all of a type made before bottle-making machines were invented in the 1890s. Research on the snuff jar suggested that it had to have been made before 1905. Research on a button suggested it was made between 1907 and 1930! Several gunshells were of a type made after 1871 and not used much after World War I (1914–1918). Do the math! What do these artifacts tell us about when folks lived there?

*Snuff jar*

From the types of artifacts found within the 2 buildings, the archaeologists concluded that the larger building was used as a home. The smaller building probably served as a small work shed. Archaeologists also found that the home had been built of sawn wood planks, and that the work shed had been built of logs. The archaeologists hypothesized that this work shed may have actually been the original home. In size and shape, it looked like many early homesteads.

It was not unusual for homesteaders to be in a hurry to build and live in a small quickly constructed building until they had time to build a better home. Then, after finishing the newer building, the homesteader could use the early building for something else, like a storage shed. This shed may not have been in use long, however. After finding burned logs, the archaeologists decided that the work shed had met a fiery fate. They were not able to say if the firebreak had been built before this fire and had failed or after the fire!

**snuff:** Tobacco that is inhaled through nose or held in mouth

Based on all of the evidence that they gathered, the archaeologists concluded that 2 Pits was the remains of a poor farm. The buildings had been small, and archaeologists found relatively few artifacts in comparison to other farmstead sites in the area. Also, most of the items found at 2 Pits were plain and had been used until they could be used no more. Evidently, the people who lived here could not afford much, and they could not waste anything. Someday archaeologists may be able to tell us more because after the site's discovery, the road construction work that would have destroyed the site was changed to avoid the area.

## Looking Back

At the beginning of the 1800s, American Indian nations controlled most of the land in Wisconsin. But by the end of the nineteenth century, Indian land was reduced to relatively small reservations in the northern part of the state. And these reservations belonged to 10 of the 11 recognized Indian Nations. The Ho-Chunk people have no reservation, but they have scattered land holdings, mostly in the western part of the state.

During the 1800s, thousands of immigrants, from the eastern and southern U.S., England, Ireland, Germany, Switzerland, Norway, Sweden, Italy, Russia, and many other countries, came to Wisconsin. These settlers came to make new lives for themselves—by mining lead, cutting lumber, and farming—and they left behind many new kinds of sites that archaeologists explore.

# Chapter 8

## Taking Care of Our Past

◆ ◆ ◆

The past is a nonrenewable resource. That means no one is creating any more Paleo-Indian campsites, or late Woodland villages, or mid-nineteenth-century logging camps. If a bulldozer plows through an archaeological site, that site and the information contained in that site are lost forever. This is why we must be so careful with the sites that we have.

Archaeologists know that they destroy portions of a site when they excavate. So they write very detailed notes on exactly where everything is found. If they don't keep track of exactly where those pieces of the puzzle go, they may never be able to figure out what the "picture" looked like.

Archaeologists' notes and artifacts are curated at universities and museums so that future archaeologists may also examine and learn from them. Archaeologists working hundreds of years from now may well have new questions about our past. Remember those mammoth bones discovered in a Kenosha County cornfield that you read about in Chapter 2? If archaeologists had not saved these bones in a museum in the 1960s, researchers in the 1990s would not have been able to examine them and discover new information on Paleo-Indian life in southern Wisconsin.

Archaeology has taught us much and can teach us a great deal more. Through archaeological research we can learn how people in Wisconsin have lived their lives over the past 12,000 years. When we study the past, we can understand the ways that we have changed and the ways that we have remained the same. We can also think about which changes were good and which were bad. When we study the past, we give ourselves a chance to make better, more informed decisions about our future.

That future is yours. But remember, to learn as *much* as we can, we must take care of Wisconsin's remaining sites. Although state and federal laws offer some protection, most archaeological sites, particularly those on private land, are not legally protected. Only the concern and work of local citizens will help guard these sites and the information they contain.

*Students listen as archaeologist Bob Birmingham explains a feature at Ft. Blue Mounds. The Dane County fort dates from the Black Hawk War in 1832.*

You now know more about archaeology than many adults! It's not just collecting arrowheads or digging up old coins. It is understanding that these things had  meaning for the people who used them. It's understanding that the things we use can also tell us— and those who follow us—important things about ourselves and about the way we live in Wisconsin.

97

# Glossary

**adapted** Changed because of a new situation

**analyze** Carefully study

**ancestors** Family members from long ago

**ancient** Very old

**archaeologists** Scientists who learn about past people by studying artifacts or objects left behind at places where people lived, worked, and played

**archaeology** Learning about past people by studying what they left in the places where they once lived

**Archaic** Time period, way of life, and American Indian group that followed the Paleo-Indians

**artifacts** Objects made by people

**atlatl** A tool used to throw a spear farther and faster

**bannerstones** Shaped pieces of stone used with atlatls

**bedrock** The solid rock that lies underneath the soils

**bombardment** Huge attack with bombs

**Cahokia** The center of the Mississippian culture, located in southern Illinois. It was a powerful city between AD 1050–1250.

**catlinite** Red pipestone found in southern Minnesota

**ceremony** Formal words, actions, or songs that mark an important occasion, such as a wedding or funeral

**chalcedony** A type of stone, good for making stone spears and arrowheads

**chert** A fine-grained type of rock that is good for making spear points and arrowheads; sometimes called flint

**chieftainess** A woman chief

**clan** Family groups with a common ancestor

**context** Exactly where artifacts are found and what is found with them

**contradicts** Is the opposite of

**cultivate** To grow for a purpose

**culture** A group of people with shared ways of life

**curation** Preserve and care for artifacts

**cylindrical** Shaped like a soda can or a tube

**dating methods** Ways that help archaeologists figure out how old things are

**decays** Rots away

**diggings** Mine sites

**dingle-style** Two buildings connected by a covered passageway

**distinctive** Easy to identify

**document** Write down and/or photograph

**Driftless Area** The part of Wisconsin never covered by glaciers, located in the southwestern part of the state

**earthworks** Very large amounts of dirt formed into different shapes

**effigy mounds** Earthen mounds made in the shapes of animals and humans about 1000 years ago, sometimes used for burials

**excavate** Carefully dig

**excavation unit** Rectangular area dug by archaeologists

**extinct** No longer exist

**features** Immovable human-made things, like house foundations or fire pits

**femur** Thigh bone

**firebreak** An area cleared of grass, shrubs, or trees in order to stop fires

**fired** Harden by heat

**flake** A sharp-edged piece of stone broken off a larger stone

**fluted points** Spear points with large grooves running up from bottom of point, used by Paleo-Indians

**fortified** To make strong and safe, protected

**Fox Indians** (see Mesquakie)

**frontier** Area on the edge of a settled region

**galena** A shiny gray mineral used to make lead

**glacier** A sheet of ice, sometimes hundreds of feet wide, that moves

**grit** Tiny bits of rock mixed with clay to make pottery

**groundstone** Stone shaped by grinding against another stone

**gunflint** Stones used to make a spark to fire old-style guns

**hammerstone** A stone used to hit another stone in order to make a tool

**harpoon** barbed spears made from bone or antler to catch fish

**hearth** fire pit

**Ho-Chunk** An American Indian tribe

**Hopewell** A Native American tradition and trade network in the Midwestern United States from about 100 BC to AD 400

**Huron** An American Indian tribe

**hypothesis** An idea that can be tested to see if it is true

**insulation** Material used to trap heat

**intact** Whole

**Ioway** An American Indian tribe

**Iroquois** An American Indian tribe

**Jesuit** Priests who were missionaries and teachers during the fur trade

**Keyhole structure** A small American Indian house in the shape of keyhole

**Kickapoo** An American Indian tribe

**lead shot** Round bullets

**longhouses** A long, cigar-shaped American Indian house shared by a number of families

**mammoth** Extinct animal related to today's elephants

**Mascouten** An American Indian tribe

**mastodon** Extinct animal related to today's elephants

**Menominee** An American Indian tribe

**Mesquakie** An American Indian tribe

**Miami** An American Indian tribe

**mica** A shiny mineral

**migrate** Move from one part of a country to another

**Mississippians** An American Indian culture found in the Midwest and southeastern United States, with strong leaders, trade and farming

**missionaries** People who hoped to convince Indians to give up their own religion and join the missionaries' church

**molars** Chewing teeth used for chewing up food

**obsidian** Volcanic glass

**Ojibwe** An American Indian tribe

**Oneida** An American Indian tribe

**Oneota** An American Indian culture in the past whose ancestors may include the Ho-Chunk and Ioway of modern times.

**oral tradition** History and stories told by one generation to the next

**Ottawa** An American Indian tribe

**Paleo-Indians** First people in the Americas

**paleontologists** Scientists who study ancient animals and plants

**peavey** A pole with a metal point on one end and a hook on the other end, used to move logs when floating down a river

**peninsula** A piece of land that sticks out from a larger mass and is almost completely surrounded by water

**petroglyph** Art made by pecking or carving out designs on a rock surface

**Petun** An American Indian tribe

**pictograph** Art made by painting a rock surface

**pike pole** A long pole with a metal point on the end, used to move logs while floating down a river

**platform mound** Large earthen mound with a flat top

**plaza** Open public area

**portage** A place where people had to carry their canoes over land

**posthole** A hole dug for a post; usually all that is left for archaeologists to see is a circle-shaped area of darker soils

**Potawatomi** An American Indian tribe

**pottery** Containers made of wet clay that are then hardened in hot fires

**quarry, quarried (past)** To dig out, dug out

**remnants** Things that are left

**Santee Dakota** An American Indian tribe

**sacred** Deserving of respect

**Sauk** An American Indian tribe

**scapulae** Shoulder blades

**seasonal** Used only part of the year

**site** Place of past human activity

**smelter** Large ovens to melt and process lead

**snuff** Tobacco that is inhaled through nose or held in mouth

**spiritual** Things that have to do with the spirit

**stockade** A line of posts used as a defensive fence

**Stockbridge-Munsee** An American Indian tribe

**stratified** Layered

**surveyed** Looked for artifacts or features

**systematic** Carefully planned

**technology** How things were made

**temper** Anything added to wet clay to prevent the clay from shrinking when fired to make pottery

**traditions** Ways of life

**treaties** Official written agreement between nations

**tributaries** A small stream that flows into a larger waterway

**unfortified** Unprotected

**Woodland** Time period, way of life, and American Indian group found in the eastern United States, defined by pottery, farming, and burial mounds

# Index

This index points to the pages where you can read about persons, places, and ideas. If you do not find the word you are looking for, try to think of another word that means about the same thing.

Sometimes the index will point to another word, like this: Boats. *See* Ships. When you see a page number in **bold** it means there is a picture or map on the page.

## A

Agriculture. *See* Farming
Archaeological sites, 6–7
   context and, 18–19
   discovery of, 8–9
   documentation and, **10**, 11–12, 96
   excavation of, 9, 11, 96
   tools used, 10
   *See also* individual site names

Archaeologists, 4
Archaic Indians, 26, **27**
   copper tools, 30–31
   diet, 35
   hunting and gathering, 28
   shelter, 30
   stone tools, 29–30, 32–33
Artifacts, 4–5, 12
Atlatls, 29, **30**

Aztalan, 47, 48–50

## B

Bannerstones, 30
Bass site, **32**–34
Bell site, **73**, 74
British, 74–75
Brown County, 20

## C

Cahokia, 47, 49
Canoes, **66**
Carbon, 7
Chalcedony, 4, 19
Climate change, 24, 28
Copper, 30–31
Crawfish River, 48
Curation, 12

## S

Salzer, Robert J., 58–60
Sherry and Gerry Logging
 Camp, 89–90
Silos, **91**
Sites. *See* Archaeological
 sites
Spear points, 18–**19**, 20,
 29, 34
 process of making, **33**
Statz site, 44–46

## T

Treaties, 82
Tremaine site, 6, 51–53
Trempealeau, 47
Two Pits site, 92–95

## U

Upper Peninsula
 (Michigan), 30
U.S. Forest Service, 89

## W

War of 1812, 75
Williamsonville, 6
Winnebago County, 74
Wisconsin River, 73
Woodland people, 36
 burial mounds and,
  40–43
 farming and, 38
 Indian Nations and,
  53–54
 pottery and, 39
 shelter and, 44–46

# Acknowledgments

It takes a real team to create a book, even a revised edition. *Digging and Discovery* benefited from the generous support of staff members of the Wisconsin Historical Society especially State Archaeologist John Broihahn. Other staff members whom we would like to acknowledge include developmental editor Elizabeth Boone, Diane Drexler, Joel Heiman, Jennifer Kolb, John Nondorf, Amy Rosebrough, and Diana Zlatanovski. Outside the Society, graphics designer Jill Bremigan created the original badger illustrations and the new cover design, Amelia Janes designed new maps, and 2econdShift Production Services, Inc. updated the interior pages to match our more recent publications. The authors send gracious thanks to them all!